People of His Presence

Fairmont Books

by
Cynthia Duggan

People of His Presence

Published by:

Fairmont Books

P.O. Box 3595
Hagerstown, MD 21742-3595
www.mcdougal.org

Fairmont Books is a ministry of The McDougal Foundation, Inc., a Maryland nonprofit corporation dedicated to spreading the Gospel of the Lord Jesus Christ to as many people as possible in the shortest time possible.

ISBN 1-884369-09-X

Printed in the United States of America
For Worldwide Distribution

Dedication

People of His Presence is the result of my heart's cry to know God ever since I was a young girl, when I met my Savior one night while kneeling at my bedside. This dedication is also a result of my love for a person who touched my life many years ago.

It has been said that there are many people who will walk into and out of your life, but only true friends will leave footprints in your heart. This is true of Iverna Tompkins, whom I was honored to meet when I was eleven years old. She visited Charleston at the invitation of my mother, who served as the president of the local Aglow chapter. I remember it as if it were yesterday. I was a young girl who longed to know and serve the God who had revealed Himself to her. I was filled with questions and longings. One day, while we were walking through the streets of historic Charleston, Iverna reached out and took my hand. She looked beyond my age, saw my heart, and spoke into my life. Through the years there have been many roads for both of us, but even in our distance I have always felt she was near me and I am extremely grateful to her.

Iverna Tompkins truly is a person of His presence, for she wears His love beautifully and demonstrates, with every breath and deed, the splendor and the grace of who He is.

I dedicate this book to her, for she saw past the "kid" I was and saw my desire for God. She deposited within me a treasure that has helped carry me forward on my journey to know and serve God.

Acknowledgments

To my husband Patrick, thank you for your continual support and love.

Seph and Hannah, thank you for being two of the best blessings from Above.

Pastor Elaine Green and the Tree of Life Church, thank you for your obedience and your seed gift, which made it possible for His promise to grow.

Martha Elizabeth Ferguson, thank you for sharing with me your beautiful gift once again. You captured my vision and my heart in the medium of color and illustration. You still amaze me.

Pastor Jan Grooms (Mom), for all your encouraging words and for listening.

Endorsements

People of His Presence will challenge the best and the worst of us to reach for that place within us where "deep calleth unto deep" and life in its fullness is truly birthed. I was challenged and motivated by the book to look once again at motives and issues of ministry that affect us all.

Sandra G. Kennedy, D.D.
Whole Life Ministries
Augusta, Georgia

The first time I met Cindy Duggan, I was stirred by her passion and zeal for God and His Church. I soon realized that she understood what it was for the Church to fulfill its prophetic destiny, to find its place in the purpose of God, and to walk in its authority by word and deed in order to effect change consistent with His plan. To accomplish our prophetic destiny, as an individual or a church body, we must not only seek His face, but abide in His presence. *People of His Presence* is an excellent guidebook to help us understand how to accomplish this goal.

Cindy clearly states that "God's presence is not for our enjoyment or for our benefit; it is for life." It is an awareness of God through relationship that you can walk in daily. I highly recommend this book to the Body of Christ and believe it will be a valuable resource for study in anyone's spiritual library.

Dee Baxter

Table of Contents

Foreword by Iverna Tompkins

I have often read in the foreword of a book, "This book is a page-turner." The meaning is, of course, that you will not want to stop reading it once you start. I can say about *People of His Presence* that it is a page-turner, not just because you will not want to put it down until you have finished reading it, but because it will challenge and enable you to turn a page in your book of life.

Cynthia Duggan is not writing theory; she is writing from both revelation and experience. From childhood through marriage and raising a family, Cynthia has had an unusual desire to know God in an intimate and purposeful way. Her pursuit of this desire resulted in the experiences and the insights she shares here. She realistically maps the way for us, with steps of truth, purity, holiness and determination.

There is no compromise here, as Cynthia encourages the reader to progress through sanctification in what Christ *does* to become a reflection of who He *is.* There is no mincing words here. The imbalance in teaching in the church world, the consequences of sin and unholiness, and the need for a personal desire to seek God are dealt with directly. But this is not a book of negatives; it is a book of hope, glorious hope, for the believers to recognize their opportunity to fulfill God's purpose for them in making them light and life to all who are in need.

Through this book, you will come to understand the words *river, fire* and *glory* as they are being used today to express the manifest presence of the Almighty. You will want to accept the rule of God and see Him face-to-face as you realize that He has lowered the scepter for our entrance so that we might come before His throne and worship.

Start turning the pages of this book, and I am sure you will start turning the pages of your life.

Iverna M. Tompkins

INTRODUCTION

As the hart panteth after the water brooks, so panteth my soul after thee, O God. My soul thirsteth for God, for the living God.

Psalm 42:1-2

From the time I was a young girl, I have walked with an unquenchable desire to know God. As I grew, I came to understand that what I was feeling was a hunger that was placed deep within me and was stirred by the hand of God. As the hunger grew, so did my search.

My pursuit to know God has taken me down many wonderful paths and many hard roads, each one unveiling a fresh aspect of God's nature.

Having a desire to know God brings longing, which often stirs us to the point of tears. It creates within us a cry that emanates from our very core and drives us to know Him, the One who dwells in the secret place.

It is with great conviction that I write *People of His Presence*. It is an attempt to express my deepest longings for the presence of God, and for what His presence is in our lives, in the Church, and in the world. Often, there are no human words that can describe this thirst; rather, it can only be expressed by groanings. It is a very real longing that is birthed in the chambers of God.

People of His Presence will take a look at the search to know God by presenting three basic truths: (1) the longing that I may know Him, (2) the journey to find Him and be like Him, and (3) the throne that is to be found in His presence.

When you seek God, you have a promise: *Seek, and ye shall find*. There is a holy God upon a holy throne waiting for you to enter His presence. When you see Him face-to-face, you will be changed.

When seeking the presence of God, it is important to ask yourself, "Why do I seek Him?" "Do I seek for blessing or for knowledge?" "Do I seek Him for power?" By answering these questions, you will discover what motivates your heart. If your motives are pure, you will find Him.

During the past several years the Church has experienced new and wonderful manifestations of the power of God. Many have been healed, delivered, restored and renewed by wonderful outpourings from God's hand. But now the question is, "What next?" Do we stop here? Of course not.

There is so much more of God that we have not yet experienced. His presence is everlasting. It is ever revealing and unveiling the many layers and facets of His nature. We are called to reflect His character in our world. Today God is revealing Himself to His Church in many fresh ways. We must not stop half-way in our journey to know Him. We must go on, entering to see Him in His fullness.

It is my desire that *People of His Presence* will express in words what you have been feeling, but have not been able to voice. Truly, God is revealing Himself, and we are to reflect Him in the midst of His people.

Let us go on to discover who God is, who we are called to be in Him, and what He has in store for those of us who yearn to be like Him.

Cynthia Duggan
Mount Pleasant, South Carolina

Part One

The Majesty

ONE

HIS GLORIOUS THRONE

In the year that king Uzziah died I saw also the Lord sitting upon a throne, high and lifted up, and his train filled the temple. Isaiah 6:1

Several years ago, some of our family came to town to visit. We took them to our local museum so they could see Charleston's history. As we walked around, looking at Indian artifacts, war memorabilia and relics from the past, I noticed one area in particular where clothing from the period was on display. There were many garments, ranging from gentlemen's dress coats to children's christening gowns. I especially noticed several wedding dresses, along with their descriptions, which dated back to the early seventeen and eighteen hundreds. Upon one of the plaques was inscribed the definition for the word *train.* It was described as "one continual piece of fabric, extending from the garment itself."

Traditionally, when a wedding dress was made, the train came from the same piece of fabric as the back panel. It was one long continual flow from the garment itself. The train often depicted the bride's station in life. If she was from a working class family, her train might only be as long as the back of her dress, but if she came from a wealthy family, her train might extend several feet behind her. If she were royalty, her train would extend the entire length of the aisle of the church. As I stood gazing at the beautiful garment, a vivid image of God's throne filled my spirit, much as Isaiah saw it.

Suddenly an awareness of God, of His holy throne, and of His habitation upon that throne came rushing upon me. I do not think God's presence had ever been so real to me as it was in that moment, and I longed for His presence as never before. I wanted to know Him in a way that I had never known Him. I felt the weight of His glory, and I wanted Him to come into every area of my life and change me.

As I stood there, looking at the trains displayed behind the glass, the truth of God's presence and who He is upon His throne filled me. I realized that His presence upon His throne is not separate from His mighty deeds. Until that moment, I had not realized how limited my understanding of God's holy presence was, and how He reaches out to me from His throne.

Today, wedding gowns come with detachable trains that can be removed to give the bride more freedom to move about unencumbered. When it comes to God's presence, we must not be guilty of detaching His presence from His throne, as if to walk around unencumbered, without responsibility and without accountability.

His Glorious Throne

The Church has been experiencing mighty winds of refreshing and renewal. But these outpourings, as wonderful as they are, should not to be our objective, nor should they be an end in themselves. Experience must not be detached from who He is upon the throne. He is far more than an experience. He is the Sovereign God upon a holy throne. As I stood in the old museum, the goodness of God overcame me, and His desire for me brought me to a decision.

Having walked with God since I was a child, I experienced His healing hand when He healed me of a degenerative eye disease. I have also seen His work in others. I have seen arms and legs grow out, I have seen individuals set free and delivered, and I have even smelled His fire, as His smoke filled auditoriums. But until that moment in the museum, I had never really seen His presence.

I knew then that I could not stop in my relationship and in my pursuit to know God. The journey to know Him had only just begun. My decision was clear, and I cried out, "I want to know You and the beauty of Your holiness," and I asked, "Touch me, and cleanse me until there is nothing left but You."

When Isaiah saw the Lord high and lifted up, it brought a cry from Isaiah's lips:

> *Woe is me! for I am undone; because I am a man of unclean lips, and I dwell in the midst of a people of unclean lips: for mine eyes have seen the King, the LORD of hosts.* Isaiah 6:5

Isaiah saw not only the throne of God but also the holiness of God. This caused him to see his own condition. We, like Isaiah, cannot cry out to see God's presence unless we are willing to take a serious look at our own spiritual condition. God never wants us to be condemned when He shows us our condition, but rather, He wants to change us.

As I gazed on the beauty of the train, and on how it fills the temple, I was enveloped by an awareness of how He longs to fill every area of our lives. I found myself in grief, repenting of the way the Church has treated His presence when He has chosen to reveal it.

God's presence is not for our enjoyment, nor for our material benefit in this life. He wants to be the very breath we breathe. He wants His Church to walk, empowered not only with the blessings of His hands, but with the revelation of who He is upon His throne. He is listening to hear our response to His invitation.

Two

Beyond Feelings

And he shewed me a pure river of water of life, clear as crystal, proceeding out of the throne of God and of the Lamb. Revelation 22:1

When we look only to what God's hands offer, we limit both God and ourselves to seeking Him only for what He offers. When we press in to see His face, however, we look past His extended hand to see Him in His fullness. Seeking God's hand is not wrong, but it will always keep the seeker at an arm's distance from Him.

God is like a diamond, in that He has many sides, or facets, to His presence. Together, these facets create the beauty and brilliance of His divine presence. There is no end to His nature. From the beginning of time the angels have looked upon God's presence, and with one voice they have cried day and night, "Holy! Holy! Holy!"

Every facet of God is holy. Every day the angels see a fresh dimension of His character, and seeing Him, they cry out and tell what they have seen — His nature. He is holy!

Allowing our hunger to be satisfied only by seeing His hand, which is what He gives us, may cause us to miss His fullness, seeing Him high and lifted up. It is imperative that we be "relationship conscious" and not only "manifestation conscious." Knowing Him means knowing all of Him.

The solemn truth found in God's revealed presence is the very fact that everything He does is based on who He is, as He pours Himself out from His throne. Who God is and what He does are not separate. There is no separation or division in God's mercy or in His judgements. He is the Lion and the Lamb upon the throne, and He rules in power and authority, with grace and mercy.

God is ever-revealing, which helps us understand why today, more than ever, He is drawing back the veil to reveal the dimensions of the eternal. It is no longer sufficient to approach His presence with a "bless-me" mentality. God's presence, whenever revealed, was and is for a purpose. He does want to bless us, but He does not want us to be motivated by cries of "Give me!"

When you cry out for God's presence, what is your motivation? What do you do when He does reveal Himself? These are tough questions, but they deserve wholehearted responses. For too long we have experienced God's presence in some meeting, only to leave with a feeling, rather than with a lasting infusion of His revealed presence. He speaks, and we forget what it was He said. Or because He chose to minister in stillness, rather than in excitement, we discount the fact that He was even there at all.

We have looked to the spectacular as a barometer, using it to indicate God's presence. Ministers often feel that something is wrong if they don't have something spectacular happening in their meetings. This view is so prevalent that conference upon conference has been held on the theme of "How to Get the Fire," despite the fact that Sunday after Sunday God's presence is felt, and one sinner after another finds the way to the altar to ask Jesus to come into his or her heart. Shame on us, when our desire for the extravagant replaces the sweetness of God's love that He wishes to give us through simple, God-centered men and women.

God's presence is life. It is not to awe us momentarily. His will is for us to walk in an awareness of Him through relationship. You do not have to run here and there to be filled with God's fire. There is a fire that you can walk with every day. It is shut up in your bones through relationship. The fire of God is not just something that He does; it is who He is. He is the refiner's fire. He is the fire-eyed God.

Whenever the fire of God is found in the midst of His people, two things need to be present, an altar and a sacrifice. God wants us to lay ourselves upon the altar as living sacrifices. His fire comes at very specific times and for very specific reasons. Let us not be content to merely see His fire burn in the midst of the camp. We must desire the fire as God burns in our midst.

New lovers experience the goose bumps stage. As wonderful as that may be, we must not base our entire relationship on what we feel, or what we don't feel. It is time for the Body of Christ to grow up. Going by what one feels is dangerous. Feelings are fickle. They change from one day to the next, and even from moment to moment. If we are going to be the people of God's presence, we must not depend on feelings, on our personality, or on what we like or dislike. We must go beyond feelings.

This world in which we live is full of counterfeit truths. All of God's truths have been counterfeited in lies that often creep back into the Church. If we do not become wise in the knowledge and in the truth of God, we will be prime candidates for deception.

Everything God does issues forth from His presence upon the throne. His throne is the center of all things past and present, as well as of things to come. As the Psalm reveals:

> *The* L*ORD* *hath prepared his throne in the heavens; and his kingdom ruleth over all.* Psalm 103:19

The throne of God is the birthplace of everything, as Jeremiah shows:

> *A glorious high throne from the beginning is the place of our sanctuary.* Jeremiah 17:12

The throne is the place where we find both mercy and judgement:

> *Mercy and truth preserve the king: and his throne is upholden by mercy.* Proverbs 20:28

I beheld till the thrones were cast down, and the Ancient of days did sit, whose garment was white as snow, and the hair of his head like the pure wool: his throne was like the fiery flame, and his wheels as burning fire. Daniel 7:9

The throne is the place where the living waters flow:

And he shewed me a pure river of water of life, clear as crystal, proceeding out of the throne of God and of the Lamb. Revelation 22:1

The throne is a place where one may find true worship:

And a voice came out of the throne, saying, Praise our God, all ye his servants, and ye that fear him, both small and great. Revelation 19:5

The throne is the place where we can find God's face:

And they shall see his face; and his name shall be in their foreheads. Revelation 22:4

God cannot be separated from His throne. When we look at the presence of God, let us not be guilty of separating it, or detaching it, from His holy presence. Our goal must be to press in and follow hard after God. David declared:

My soul followeth hard after thee: thy right hand upholdeth me. Psalm 63:8

People of His Presence

When we pursue God, we can rest in the fact that His hand is always there, upholding us through the journey. All the while we are pursuing Him, He is there, drawing us to Himself. We journey not alone; *deep calleth unto deep.* The waters ripple and we respond. It is in our response that we find the One for whom our soul longs. Never stop halfway in your pursuit of God. Do not be content to see anything less than all of Him — His feet, His hands, His mouth and His eyes — for He is altogether beautiful.

Three

Beyond Manifestations

Then said I, Woe is me! for I am undone; because I am a man of unclean lips, and I dwell in the midst of a people of unclean lips: for mine eyes have seen the King, the LORD of hosts. Isaiah 6:5

The prophet Isaiah knew and understood who it was he was seeing upon the throne. This tells me that he walked in a relationship with God. So many times we miss God, or what He is revealing, simply because we do not see through the eyes of relationship. Relationship is the key to revelation.

At the time of Isaiah's visitation, the Lord was calling him up to a higher place of responsibility, accountability and relationship. The visitation had a purpose. It wasn't to give him something to talk about; it wasn't to build up his congregation; nor was it to send him forth with awe. God had a specific mandate for Isaiah, and if he was to carry out that mandate, it was essential that he fully see, hear and experience God.

I believe God is calling all His people to a higher place of relationship, responsibility and accountability. He desires to expand Himself in us, so that we may walk as a people who are rich in the knowledge of *Christ in [us], the hope of glory.*

Children often whine. They whine about what they're told to do, about what they want, and about what they think they need. It is time for us to walk as mature sons and daughters of God, not wavering in our purpose, knowing who we are in Christ.

I once heard Mary Ann Brown say, "You are only young once, but you can choose to stay immature your entire life." The truth of that statement made an impact on me, and I began to see areas in my life I was choosing to hold on to, things that were keeping me from maturing and reaching a place of obedience.

God isn't looking for those who are self-motivated, self-indulgent or self-promoting. Jesus is our example in this regard. He always did the will of His Father in Heaven, never once refusing to do what His Father commanded.

Jesus never grumbled or complained about the will of His Father. He never questioned His Father's will, nor did He question God's purposes. Jesus knew what He was sent to do, and He willingly obeyed.

I disagree with those who depict Jesus as questioning God's purpose when He was in the garden, when He asked the Father to let the bitter cup pass from Him. In everything that Jesus did, He provided an example. I do not believe that He was teaching us to question the will of the Father, but instead, how to surrender our will to the Father's in our moments of greatest struggle.

The Church will soon experience one of the greatest outpourings it has known, but I am afraid that we are looking toward that outpouring only for the signs, the wonders and the manifestations it will bring. In Scripture, whenever there was a great sign or manifestation of God's presence, it carried with it a purpose. God isn't manifesting Himself in our midst just to overwhelm us, or to leave us awestruck. Rather, He is manifesting Himself so that He can impart to us a revelation of who He is.

Whenever God manifests Himself through fire, He isn't simply trying to keep us warm. Fire is a manifestation of His person. He is the wind, the water, the oil and the glory. He is healing, joy and laughter. These are not by-products of His working, nor are they something He does for attention. They are His essence. We have become so accustomed to hearing about His works that we have forgotten they are really part of His nature. Unless God is revealed to us, we will falter when we try to reveal Him to someone else. To be useful to Him, we will need to look past the vehicle of His expression and see the revealed God.

Moses was called to the top of a mountain by an angel who appeared in a bush that seemed to be on fire (see Exodus 3:2). Upon seeing this, Moses turned aside and found that even though the bush was on fire, it wasn't consumed. The Lord then called to Moses from the burning bush, and Moses, upon hearing God's voice, said, *"Here am I"* (see Exodus 3:3-4). The vehicles God used to speak to Moses were an angel, a fire, and a bush. God wanted Moses to see the burning bush. This was His method of gaining Moses' attention. Once He has gained our attention, God always looks to see our response. In Scripture, He used many things to get man's attention. There were the plagues of Egypt (see Exodus 7-12), water coming from a rock (see Exodus 17:6), a speaking donkey (see Numbers 22:28) and a bright light (see Acts 9:3), just to name a few. God is a revealing God. He uses many things to reveal Himself to us.

Despite the fact that God uses great manifestations to get our attention, He never intended for us to camp around His manifestations. His desire is that we stop and look, and then see Him, and that we continue from there into a deeper knowledge of His person.

Reflections of God's presence are increasing within the Church. As wonderful as these reflected views may be, however, they are not the end. They are only a bridge to help us see another portion of God's nature.

The winds of God are blowing upon the Church. These winds, again, are reflections of Him. Whenever we experience the winds of God, we must look to the source. Wind, by definition, is described as "any stream of air that is produced by a bellows or a fan, or by breathing, movement, or force." Wind always has an eye, or a source. The source of the spiritual winds we are experiencing is God:

> *Who hath ascended up into heaven, or descended? who hath GATHERED THE WIND in his fists? who hath*

> *bound the waters in a garment? who hath established all the ends of the earth? what is his name, and what is his son's name, if thou canst tell?* Proverbs 30:4

God alone directs the wind. All the elements, whether they are the wind, the fire or the rain, are not —in and of themselves —the person of God, but rather, they give us an insight into and an understanding of His person. It is He that we must come to know first.

Several years ago, God began speaking to our church through prophetic song. He spoke of the mighty winds that would blow, of a shaking and a pulling up of foundations. We considered that this would be something God would do in the realm of the Spirit, and we failed to seek Him for more understanding. We were content to see it in the way we understood it. Little did we know that God was stretching us and teaching us to go beyond our perception to what He was actually trying to tell us.

Several weeks after God began to speak this way in service after service, He spoke to our senior pastor and told her to cook several pounds of potatoes and fry four chickens and two hams. Then He instructed her to call off services. Within hours, we received news that Charleston was about to be hit with a category-three hurricane.

During the weeks after the hurricane, we went back and listened to tape after tape of God's instructions concerning what was coming. It was amazing how accurate God had been, if only we had had ears to hear. He had been preparing us for weeks, and we had not realized it.

We learned a great lesson, one that we have never forgotten. So often, we miss what God is actually doing and saying because we're content to look at it through our own understanding, instead of seeking God for His perfect plan. If we are going to be a people of God's presence, we must learn to look at life through the eyes of His eternal plan. We must see that He is depositing Himself within us each time He reveals Himself in our midst. He wants us to go beyond what's comfortable, beyond the familiar, to the point of absolute trust.

One of the reasons we don't trust God completely is that we don't really know Him well enough. When I was a young girl, I played a game with my father on the back of his pickup truck. I would turn around and yell, "Catch me, Daddy!" and fall blindly into his arms, knowing he was always there and would catch me. Why is it that we don't have this same assurance when it comes to our heavenly Father? We cry to Him, "Carry me! Catch me!" But then we keep one eye open, just to see if He's actually there.

The Scriptures teach that in these last days, *"darkness shall cover the earth, and gross darkness the people"* (Isaiah 60:2). If we can't trust beyond what we're able to see, we'll be overtaken by the darkness. God wants us to be His hands, outstretched to this dying and hurting world. We are His priests, and are called to touch the infirmities of His people, but if we don't have a living knowledge of, and a relationship with, God, we will be of little or no effect. We will not be able to offer a clear word of direction to others if we do not know where we are headed ourselves.

Beyond Manifestations

Everything we experience in life points us to God and prepares us for what lies ahead. I had a very lonely childhood. I spent many hours alone, with the feeling that I was swimming upstream. Little did I know, at the ages of twelve and thirteen, that God was preparing me for something I would experience twenty years later.

When I was seventeen, God spoke to me and told me that He would give me a rod of iron in my back. In my youth, I thought, "Great! Thank You." I had the concept of God opening my back and giving me all the strength I would need — instantly. I didn't understand that the rod would grow inch-by-inch and through much difficulty, much rejection and many misunderstandings. If I had known then that it would grow through great hurt and the circumstances of life, I might not have been so quick to say thank you.

Nevertheless, I wouldn't give up or erase one portion of the truth and the security these experiences have worked in me. All of this taught me one thing, to press in and to find myself in God, and not seek for man's approval.

When we learn to see God through the eyes of relationship, everything He does takes on a different perspective. Because Isaiah was a man who walked in relationship, he didn't miss what it was that God was trying to reveal to him. When he saw the Lord, he cried out:

> *Then said I, Woe is me! for I am undone; because I am a man of unclean lips, and I dwell in the midst of a people of unclean lips: for mine eyes have seen the King, the LORD of hosts.* Isaiah 6:5

Seeing the King, the Lord of Hosts, caused Isaiah to see his own condition and the condition of those around him. If we desire to be a people of God's holy presence, we must also be willing to see our own condition and the condition of things around us. Holding on to anything that is not God's will for our lives will only keep us from His throne.

God doesn't show us our condition of unrighteousness to condemn us, but to change us into His image. If we're carrying baggage — things that aren't pleasing to the Father — we won't be able to reflect the image of God. We have to be willing to let go of everything that isn't pleasing to Him.

God had a mandate for Isaiah, and a goal for him to accomplish, but first he needed to become what God needed him to be. How many times do we miss being used by God because we refuse to let Him mold and fashion us into the vessels He needs?

When we cry out to know God, we must be willing to be changed into the image that He gives us. Often, we miss God because we want to stay in the same place and in the same condition we were in before He came.

So many times, in churches all across America, God chooses to reveal Himself to a particular body of believers during a particular moment in time, only to have them go on, as if nothing happened, following their same agenda or program. It often happens that when God speaks in the midst of His people, we are asked to be seated without an acknowledgment that He has even uttered a sound. The person in charge of the meeting goes ahead without any response, without embracing the message, and without any worship or any demonstration of thankfulness of heart.

As a parent, I expect my children to acknowledge my voice. I look for some response that shows they've heard me. If they're wise, their response will be one of obedience. If they choose to ignore me, they will meet with the consequences.

If my children choose to disregard or disobey my voice, they are met with a strong or stern admonishment. When the Father speaks, do we think He expects anything less from us? Sometimes we cannot see past the vessel, or the instrument, that He chooses to use, and it places us in a position that causes us to miss God. He is simply looking for a yielded and obedient heart; He is not a respecter of persons.

Seldom do the qualifications that God has established for a vessel He will use match those that we bring to Him. He looks for things that are more important than pedigree, education and economic standards. He looks on our hearts. Things that may disqualify you in the sight of man often qualify you in the sight of God. After all, He chose a murderer (Moses) to deliver His people, an adulterer (David) to be king, and a slayer of Christians (Saul/Paul) to be one of the greatest theologians of the Bible. God does not look at what you are, but rather, what you are willing to become, in His hands.

In much of the Church today there is a game being played. It concerns those who are considered to be "in" and those who are considered to be "out." Big names, big crowds, and big price tags are part of the game. Ministries and individuals are demanding high-priced honorariums, ritzy hotels, limousines and even personal physical trainers, and they now travel with an entourage of bodyguards. I don't believe that God is pleased with this display. Whatever happened to the scripture:

> *I therefore, the prisoner of the Lord, beseech you that ye walk worthy of the vocation wherewith ye are called, with all lowliness and meekness, with longsuffering, forbearing one another in love; endeavouring to keep the unity of the Spirit in the bond of peace.*
>
> Ephesians 4:1-3

"Ministry" has become a big business, and I believe that this makes the Father weep. While it is true that men and women of God are to be taken care of, I don't believe God is pleased with many of the things that are being done in the name of ministry. I don't know who should be blamed more for this conduct. Should it be the Body, for not taking proper care of God's men and women, and thus forcing ministers to adapt certain behavior, or should we blame those leaders who feel they deserve special attention because of their anointing and the favor of God upon their lives? Whatever the case may be, the resulting behavior is an embarrassment to the name of the Lord.

God wants us to be a *People of His Presence,* bearing all things in humility, showing forth His nature and not the medals of our achievements. He is looking for ministers who are more concerned about people seeing Him than about their seeing the vessel He uses.

There are serious days ahead for the Church. The

world is dying quickly. Heaven's doors are bulging as Jesus anxiously awaits the word from His Father: "Go!" It's time to get down to the business at hand — God's Kingdom. It is time to understand that ministry has nothing to do with us, but everything to do with God in us. If the world looks at me, and all they see is "me," then I've failed. It's not important who I am, but who God is in me.

Jesus, who is the Anointed One, was meek and always pointed individuals to the Father. He had every right to be looked upon Himself, for He holds all authority and all anointing. Compared to Jesus, we hold but a thimbleful, yet we walk around as if we are important.

God's Kingdom is at hand, and our purpose is to walk, revealing the King, the Lord of Hosts, who dwells on the throne. There is no place for self on His throne. Only the Lord, whose name is Jesus, can sit there.

Part Two

The Longing

Four

The Cry for Relationship

Lord, Lord, I want to hold Your hand.
Lord, Lord, I want to kiss You sweetly.
Lord, Lord, I love You.
Lord, Lord, I want to run with You.
Lord, Lord, I want to walk with You.
Lord, Lord, I want to see Your face.
Lord, Lord, I love You.
Lord, Lord, I want to kiss You sweetly.

by Seph Duggan (my son)
Age 8

Regardless of age, whether you are young or old, there's a cry going forth from God, calling you to know and love Him. This hunger for knowing Him, which He has given you, is a hunger that began long ago in His heart, even before the foundation of the Earth. God has always desired to have a people in whom He could deposit Himself and who would walk, reflecting His image.

In the beginning, God made man, and in creating him, God wove Himself into man's very being. God intended for man to walk in a relationship with his Creator, reflecting His presence and image. When Adam and Eve ate of the fruit of the forbidden tree, they removed themselves from that relationship. This separation caused them to walk as individuals, rather than as God's image on Earth.

Their disobedience didn't change God's desire for them. He still wanted a people who would walk in a true relationship and covenant with Him, reflecting His image. To accomplish this task, God put in motion a divine plan that was designed to draw man, and keep him by God's side. He accomplishes this by placing a hunger and thirst within man, especially designing this hunger to draw man to His side. He places within man a desire that cannot be satisfied until he is locked in a divine embrace. This is a longing that keeps man stirred to the place of seeking. It keeps man discontent with anything and everything until He turns to God.

Scripture reveals to us that God is a jealous God. What is He jealous of? He's jealous for you. One of the simplest truths is that God is for us. He is willing and ready to deposit in us, all of Himself. God formed man for Himself. Why were we created? We were created to glorify God. For this reason, He sent His Son to redeem us and return us to that place of relationship that we lost in the fall, so that we can reflect His image.

In the days of old, God told Moses to build a tabernacle in which He could dwell and be close to His people.

This was fine for a while, but it wasn't God's ultimate plan. God wanted man. He wasn't content to dwell among men in only a tent. He wanted to dwell inside of each individual. When we think of the cry for relationship, we tend to think in terms of its coming only from us, that we alone are responsible for the pursuit of relationship. The cry for relationship, however, comes from the heart of God.

Perhaps one of the reasons it's so hard for us to comprehend that God is the One who first seeks us, is that we cannot see Him wanting us. We cannot comprehend that He actually longs to spend time with us.

I have often pondered this question: What does God get for all of His suffering and the time He spends drawing us, molding us and teaching us? I know what I get out of it: blessings, healing, provision, comfort, joy, etc. But what does God get? Then I realized: He gets me. When I saw how much He truly desired me, loved me and wanted me, it changed how I approached everything. Every covenant and plan that He has made and every task that He has undertaken has me in mind.

So, what does He get out of it? He gets a bride! He gets a people who are committed and dedicated to Him, one hundred percent. Scripture reveals that it was God who first loved us. In fact, love did not even begin with man; it began in the heart of the One who created man and desired to have companionship with him. Love is not something God simply gives or offers; love is who He is. Everything He does is backed by this very fact. He is a relationship God. He is a covenant-making God.

Time after time, the Scriptures reveal the drawing nature of God. In the establishment of His covenants He tells us to come to Him:

> *Incline your ear, and COME UNTO ME: hear, and your soul shall live; and I will make an everlasting covenant with you, even the sure mercies of David.*
> Isaiah 55:3

> *COME UNTO ME, all ye that labour and are heavy laden, and I will give you rest. Take my yoke upon you, and learn of me; for I am meek and lowly in heart: and ye shall find rest unto your souls. For my yoke is easy, and my burden is light.* Matthew 11:28-30

> *If any man thirst, let him COME UNTO ME, and drink.* John 7:37

The cry for relationship is not a cry that we alone offer up. It is also a cry that comes from the heart of God toward man.

Is this something we deserve?

No.

Does that matter to God?

No.

God chooses only to see us through the precious blood of His dear Son. Man deserved death, but Christ paid the ultimate debt so that we, by faith, could walk in relationship with and be found in God.

You and I have many relationships. Some of them are rather formal and limited to a handshake or a greeting.

Other relationships are based on friendship. This is reflected by warm tones of affection and laughter, and in heart-to-heart embraces. Then there is the relationship of intimacy. It is the strongest of all because with it there is a binding covenant. An intimate relationship reflects the strength, the commitment, and the passion that can only come through face-to-face contact.

Just as natural human relationships produce a reflection, so does our relationship with God. When God was revealing to John His judgements against the seven churches, there was one that stood out — the judgement against Ephesus. This is a classic example of a lack of relationship or a lack of reflection.

The church of Ephesus was growing. The Ephesian believers had shown patience in their labor, and they did not entertain evil. They judged the false apostles and did not faint in the ministry. However, when Jesus looked for signs of a relationship, He did not see a reflection. He said:

> *Nevertheless I have somewhat against thee, because thou hast left thy first love.* Revelation 2:4

By all appearances, Ephesus would have been a church on the right track. The people seemed to be doing everything right, but when it came to God, they needed something more substantial than just the ability to do things correctly.

I have often pondered God's judgement in light of these two words: *first love.* One day, as I was studying, I went to my husband and asked him what he thought of this term. He explained his understanding of first love in light of relationships and society's definition. I continued to probe until he sat back and asked, "Why? What's up with all these questions?" He could tell that something was on my mind.

I had been thinking about friendships I had had before meeting Patrick, and I was trying to analyze why none of them had led to love and a covenant relationship. I had felt an infatuation for some, but it came one day and left the next.

With Patrick it was different. I could remember the exact day that I knew I was in love with him, and from that moment on, everything changed. I waited for his calls. I couldn't let a day pass without hearing his voice. I sought to please him, and I wanted to spend every hour of every day with him. I wanted to find out everything about him. In fact, I ached to know him more as each day passed.

What stands out the most in my memory, however, is the fact that others could see my love for Patrick. My love and longing produced a reflection that was clearly visible. The love that I had for him compelled me to spend the rest of my life with him. It brought me to the place of marriage and covenant.

Now that Patrick and I have been married for eleven years, we have to work at it to keep our first love alive. We have grown comfortable with each other, and the winds of life have blown us in many directions. It's a challenge to keep the flames of passion alive. Husbands and wives must be careful not to get so caught up with all of life's ups and downs that familiarity and comfortableness replace compassion's tender words. Just as husbands and wives must strive to keep alive the passion that once drew them to each other, so we must contend to keep the first love in our relationship with God.

As I thought of the judgement against Ephesus in light of my first love for Patrick, I could see what God was looking for. He was looking for a hunger, a longing, and a cry that comes from an ache for intimacy. David knew this cry. He spoke of intimacy when he said:

> *When thou saidst, Seek ye my face; my heart said unto thee, Thy face, LORD, will I seek.* Psalm 27:8

It is this cry that takes us beyond any superficial relationship and carries us into the very chamber of God.

The hour of truth has come. God is calling forth those who earnestly desire to know Him in His fullness. If we desire a true relationship, we will surrender our wills, casting aside all distractions, time restraints and excuses. Our satisfaction comes in finding ourselves filled with the desire to be touched by God, knowing that only He can satisfy, complete, and fill us up.

He wants us to walk each and every day with the anticipation of discovering something new. He wants us to seek after Him with everything that is within us. He wants us *"to ravish [Him] with [just] one of [our] eyes"!*

> *Thou hast ravished my heart, my sister, my spouse; thou hast ravished my heart with one of thine eyes, with one chain of thy neck.* Song of Solomon 4:9

The longing that God places deep within us is not a longing that can be satisfied by a casual encounter. It is a passion that burns to know Him intimately:

> *Let him kiss me with the kisses of his mouth: for thy love is better than wine.* Song of Solomon 1:2

When we cry to know God, we are not to be content with any experience *("wine").* We must not be satisfied until He has pressed His lips to ours. This is the cry of the bride for her bridegroom. This is the cry of longing. No handshake will do; she wants all there is of the one who is her heart's desire.

From the beginning of time, we have been drawn to God. He does not want us to be content with anything less than His all. He does not withhold any part of Himself from us. If we truly seek Him, we shall find Him, and when we find Him, we shall become like Him.

Five

Those Who Worship

With my whole heart have I sought thee: O let me not wander from thy commandments. Thy word have I hid in mine heart, that I might not sin against thee. Make me to understand the way of thy precepts: so shall I talk of thy wondrous works.

It is good for me that I have been afflicted; that I might learn thy statutes. The law of thy mouth is better unto me than thousands of gold and silver. Thy hands have made me and fashioned me: give me understanding, that I may learn thy commandments.

Thy word is a lamp unto my feet, and a light unto my path. Psalm 119:10-11, 27, 71-73 and 105

David was a man who constantly cried out for the light of God's presence to penetrate his life. He depended on the presence of God to direct him, to keep him, and to sustain him. He knew that without the presence of God, he was nothing, and without God he didn't have life. God is looking and listening to hear the same cry that David made, from His people today. He is anxiously awaiting the sound of intimacy, the sound of His people crying, "I am nothing apart from You. You are the very breath I breathe!"

David knew how important it was for his path to be lit. He grew up as a young shepherd in the hills, watching over his flock. I'm sure he walked many nights alone in the dark. Just as David was well acquainted with loneliness in the natural, he also become a man acquainted with the lonely path of rejection. He spent much of his life fleeing and alone.

In David's youth, Saul hunted him. When David became the king, his enemies hated him. In his darkest hour of sin, he felt that God had abandoned him. Whatever his circumstances in life, David knew the importance of God's presence and never wanted to be without it. He longed to stay continually in the presence of God, and didn't want to lose sight of God and didn't want God to lose sight of him.

When we long for God, we are destined for change. The Scriptures teach us that when we see Him, *"we shall be like him"* (1 John 3:2). This points to change. We are *"changed ... from glory to glory"* as we look upon Christ (2 Corinthians 3:18). This means that you cannot see God unless you're willing to be changed.

To David, relationship, God's presence, and God's commandments went hand in hand:

Those Who Worship

With my whole heart have I sought thee: O let me not wander from thy commandments. Psalm 119:10

David knew that to cry out for God meant embracing all of God. God's commandments are God's laws, and His laws direct men in all truth. When David longed for God and His commandments, David knew he would come face to face with the truth and be changed. David knew this, and he knew that when he longed for God, He would come in all of His truth and change every area of David's life.

David knew what it meant to be indwelt with the presence of God. He also knew what it meant for God to withhold His presence because of sin. David didn't want to be without God's presence, so he continually yearned for God to survey his life and keep him free of sin, and from sin's entanglements. David wrote:

Search me, O God, and know my heart: try me, and know my thoughts: and see if there be any wicked way in me, and lead me in the way everlasting.
Psalm 139:23-24

The prophet Daniel stated:

He revealeth the deep and secret things ... and the light dwelleth with him. Daniel 2:22

God is omniscient. He is all-knowing. There is absolutely nothing that escapes Him. *"He knoweth what is in the darkness."* His knowledge and wisdom are perfect.

He never fails, never changes, never overlooks, and never makes a mistake. As the writer of Hebrews stated:

> *Neither is there any creature that is not manifest in his sight: but all things are naked and opened unto the eyes of him with whom we have to do.*
>
> Hebrews 4:13

Throughout Scripture, God's Word is often referred to as a light. Jesus Himself is referred to as *"the light of the world."* The light of God's presence, when revealed, shows forth all truth. When David cried to know God, he cried out for continual truth to be a part of his life. We should not cry out for God unless we are willing to be exposed in His light and in His truth.

When we long for relationship, we are also crying out to know the revealed Word of God. Jesus was, and is, the Word made flesh. Longing for relationship causes us to embrace the truth. Without the acceptance of truth we cannot be changed; we will simply live in our current state.

Truth is always easier to receive when it is presented in a way that wraps it in relationship. Personally, I can accept the hardest of truths if I know there is love. So, God draws us, wraps us in His love, presents His truth to us, and changes us into His likeness.

The light of His presence often reminds me of a makeup mirror. On one side there is a regular mirror, and on the other a magnifying mirror. When I use a soft light with the regular side of the mirror facing me, my face looks smooth and clear. When I flip the mirror, however, and turn on the bright lights, I see the real picture, and it's not like the one I imagined.

God wants us to flip over the "mirror" and let the light of His true presence shine. David cried:

> *Thou knowest my downsitting and mine uprising, thou understandest my thought afar off. Thou compassest my path and my lying down, and art acquainted with all my ways. For there is not a word in my tongue, but, lo, O LORD, thou knowest it altogether.*
>
> Psalm 139:2-4

It's one thing to long for God, and quite another to accept Him after you've found Him. Knowing that God knows everything about you and embracing the truth He reveals is often a difficult process. He knows our coming in and our going out, but to let Him deal with all of our hidden areas and change them, as we look boldly into the brilliant mirror of His truth, is a great struggle.

David went to great lengths to cover up his affair with Bathsheba, but God wanted to expose his sin, so He sent a messenger to say, *"Thou art the man."* The fact that God is all-knowing is a truth that people often face with discomfort. Sooner or later, we have to come face-to-face with our desires, thoughts and actions that we have hidden from others, and maybe even from ourselves, but not from God. His hope is for us to come to this realization sooner rather than later, remembering that time is short. True relationship is grounded in truth.

Our society is immersed in deceit, and it has penetrated everything from the White House to the brick house. Truth's light will shine forth, cutting away every sign of deception. God's presence will blaze as men and women who are filled with the Spirit of truth stand for what is right. In God's eyes, the right thing isn't always what it may be in man's eyes or in man's way of thinking. As Christians, we are not called to be "politically correct," nor are we called to be "politically incorrect," but we are called to be "scripturally correct." This means that we will stand in the true Word of God and not in the counsel of the ungodly, or even in the counsel of those who are called "wise" by this world.

I used to love a good debate, but I've come to the place where I no longer see the value of debating politics, the economy or religion. I'm only interested in what is rooted and grounded in God's principles. I do not want to hear theory, intellect or opinion if it's not based on God's Word and grounded in relationship.

The principles of God's Kingdom seldom agree with the principles of this world. So much of the world's ideas and concepts have filtered into the Church that I've often wondered what the Church would do if we were faced with a man who had been stripped, wounded and left for dead on the side of the road (see Luke 10:30-37). Would we bother ourselves with the poor victim? Or would we say, "Leave it to the groups that help 'those kinds of people'"? Would we stand there and debate the problems of welfare in our society or discuss the tax laws that concern the poor? This world's opinions should not sway us from the truth.

Truth isn't just a way that God uses to reveal our inner motives. It's also a key element in worship that He longs for:

Those Who Worship

But the hour cometh, and now is, when the true worshippers shall worship the Father in spirit and in truth: for the Father seeketh such to worship him. God is a Spirit: and they that worship him must worship him in spirit and in truth. John 4:23-24

When Jesus spoke these words, He was speaking to the woman at the well. He knew that she walked in limited understanding. Her knowledge and relationship had been based on the worship that her ancestors established. She said to Him:

Our fathers worshipped in this mountain; and ye say, that in Jerusalem is the place where men ought to worship. John 4:20

Jesus knew that this woman was a Samaritan and that it would take a lot for her to leave the worship of her forefathers. So He looked into the depths of her soul and imparted truth, that Jew and Samaritan would worship the one true God together:

The same came for a witness, to bear witness of the Light, THAT ALL MEN THROUGH HIM MIGHT BELIEVE. John 1:7

Jesus was showing the Samaritan woman that she couldn't hold on to religion, in any form, simply because it was what her family believed. Just because Grandma and Granddad worshiped in one way does not need to keep you from finding your own relationship with God.

Entrance into the Kingdom of God isn't made through any denomination. When we go to be with the Father, He's not going to ask us which denomination we belonged to down here. He will look beyond man-made "badges" and see our hearts. He will be looking to see if there are any signs of life — His life.

Jesus helped the Samaritan woman to see that He was the Messiah, and to see that He was more important than the mountain where people might worship. Jesus is not limited to a particular building. He's alive, and He's Spirit. This was, and is, the truth that He still wants to reveal today.

The Father seeks those who will worship Him, those who are not concerned about worshiping in a certain building, using a particular ceremony, reciting a specific creed, adhering to an exact denomination, or maintaining an explicit tradition. He wants the heart of man.

The disciples, upon seeing Jesus talking to this woman, were confused. Why would He talk to a heathen? Jesus had to explain to them that His salvation is for all men:

> *Jesus saith unto them, My meat is to do the will of him that sent me, and to finish his work. Say not ye, There are yet four months, and then cometh harvest? behold, I say unto you, Lift up your eyes, and look on the fields; for they are white already to harvest. And he that reapeth receiveth wages, and gathereth fruit unto life eternal: that both he that soweth and he that reapeth may rejoice together. And herein is that say-*

ing true, One soweth, and another reapeth. I sent you to reap that whereon ye bestowed no labour: other men laboured, and ye are entered into their labours.

John 4:34-38

When Jesus said to Peter *"Upon this rock I will build my church"* (Matthew 16:18), He wasn't forming a denomination. He was speaking of the Rock in whom Peter had trusted. There is a huge deception that has been sown concerning this one scripture. The context of the scripture is that Simon Barjona (Peter) has just revealed that Jesus is *"the Christ, the Son of the living God."* This was the truth: Jesus, the Christ, is the Rock that the Church would be built upon. It was against this truth — that the Church is established upon Jesus the Rock — that the gates of Hell would not prevail.

Please note, I am not against denominations. However, I am against the concept, which many hold: "I was born a Baptist (Methodist, Episcopal or Catholic) and I'll die as such." It's dangerous to make a denomination your life's source, rather than grounding yourself in a relationship with Jesus. When Jesus draws us, He does not draw us to a form of religion, but to Himself. He's not a Methodist, an Episcopal or a Fundamentalist. He is God, the Savior of all mankind.

On the day that Jesus spoke to the woman at the well, the disciples didn't yet walk in a fullness of the knowledge of the truth. Jesus had to break down their barrier of human understanding. I believe the same is happening today. He is breaking down all of the barriers that have kept us from worshiping Him in Spirit and in truth.

He's calling us to be one body. Relationship with the Beloved means we are all connected to each other.

One of the greatest causes of division is that each group of believers has its own agenda. Each has its own set of rules, its own interpretations and its own prejudices. When the disciples questioned Jesus concerning the woman, they were showing signs of prejudice. Jesus had to reveal to them that it was through Him alone that every person would be saved. It is impossible to have true relationship without truth.

Truth brings illumination. Jesus told His disciples that they were the light of the world. Jesus taught them concerning His Kingdom principles:

> *Ye are the light of the world. A city that is set on an hill cannot be hid. Neither do men light a candle, and put it under a bushel, but on a candlestick; and it giveth light unto all that are in the house. Let your light so shine before men, that they may see your good works, and glorify your Father which is in heaven.*
>
> Matthew 5:14-16

"A city set on a hill" is a beacon for all to see. Sailors at sea use cities set on hillsides as a reference point to guide them. In Charleston, there is a historic church located downtown on Church Street. One of the reasons it's historic is because of the function it served during the Civil War. Often, during the war, the North used this church to mark the middle of the city, and would shoot their cannons toward its tall white steeple. Because of the repeated fire, the townspeople decided to paint the steeple

black, so it could not be spotted by the enemy and used as an easy target.

I've often thought of this in relation to the Church. Jesus has called the Church to be a landmark, a beacon for all to see. If we're going to be a light of truth, for everyone to see, we cannot have two faces. The Scriptures teach clearly that you cannot be one who seeks to please men and still please God. If you hold on to your own rights, you may miss the truth that the Spirit of God, within you, would work in your life.

David's appeal to know God was not an idle cry. He cried out to know God and be known by God. The cry for relationship is where we start, and the embrace of relationship is where we are changed. True relationship is formed and established when we are willing to embrace truth and lay down everything that would keep us from His side.

Part Three

The Journey

SIX

BEYOND THE CHAMBER

How amiable are thy tabernacles, O LORD of hosts! My soul longeth, yea, even fainteth for the courts of the LORD: my heart and my flesh crieth out for the living God. Psalm 84:1-2

One day I was in worship when the Spirit of the Lord spoke to my heart concerning relationship. I immediately felt an urgency for the hour in which we are living. In a moment, I felt my relationship with the Lord being judged, and I felt the weight of my responsibility to walk out that relationship.

As I stood in the moment of truth, I became overwhelmed with the awareness of the high place to which we are called. I knew immediately that arriving there would involve a walk in complete relationship, through trust.

Then I felt God turn and take a step away. Soon it felt as though I was standing alone. I could no longer see His face, only His back. I followed Him.

I ached to see His face. I wanted to look into His eyes. I wanted to hold on to Him in the relationship of the chamber, but somehow I knew the relationship that I had become so accustomed to had somehow changed. There was a destiny, a plan, and it involved me depending upon the relationship that I had spent so much time building, as I sought the Lord's face in the chamber.

The Father is taking us up to a higher degree of relationship. It is a relationship that is secure, and not one that is based on feelings. It is centered around a living knowledge of who God is.

When you have spent time with God, face-to-face, you come and are confident of His favor even when He seems to be far away. The Hebrew word for face-to-face is *paniym.* It encompasses the intimate relationship that exists between two parties by whom a covenant has been established.

God has turned, and is walking forward with a determined stride, but once a covenant is made it is not broken just because the parties are distant. We should not lose heart. I am confident that God's face is always present and that He continues to draw us into His chamber so that we can spend time with Him in a lover's embrace.

However, He knows that we cannot stay in this place of embrace. We must take our love to the highways and byways, and we must not fear. God is with us. When people are in love, it shows. Relationship is evident in a person's life. God wants us to be a people who wears His love for all to see.

In the days of old, a man's garment depicted what, or who, he was. The priests wore a particular garment and the prophets wore another, called a mantle. Wherever they went, people could recognize them by their garments. Elisha, after he had received Elijah's mantle, was seen coming toward Jericho. When the sons of the prophets saw him, they said, *"The spirit of Elijah doth rest on Elisha"* (2 Kings 2:15). (Elijah was filled with the Spirit of God.) When the Spirit of the Lord rests upon us, it is visible to those who are around us.

Relationship takes us down many paths. Some are smooth, but the majority of them are very rocky. It is often in the place of difficulty that true relationship is developed. When things are easy, our true identity is often hidden from view. The same is true with God.

When things are easy, we tend to put God on the back burner, but in a moment of difficulty, we seek Him. Many of us would never have known God if He hadn't made Himself real to us through adversity. This is frequently the place where we start. It's not, however, a place in which we are to stay. God doesn't want us to seek Him only because of adversity. Rather, He wants us to seek to know Him just because He's our Bridegroom and we love Him.

Relationship with God takes many forms. I want to discuss three of these, which I believe are keys to unlocking the rich truth of the knowledge of God upon His throne.

The first relationship is that with the BELOVED. With

this relationship, we are given a heart transplant. When we are born into this world, we are born in the likeness of Adam. We are in relationship with the kingdom of darkness, and not with the Kingdom of God. Our spirits are dead and in need of rebirth. There is a veil of flesh that must be torn away. But when we come to know Jesus in our hearts, we receive the adoption of sonship, and we call Him *"Abba, Father"* (Romans 8:15)

God, in turn, marries us to the Word of God, who is Jesus. He is and was the *"Word made flesh."* When we receive Him into our hearts, He comes, applying the written Word of God. The written Word of God acts as a two-edged sword, dividing that veil of flesh that separates us from God (see Ephesians 6:17 and Hebrews 4:12). When the Word of God is applied in your life, as truth, it marries you to the brethren.

This brings us to our second relationship: that with the BRETHREN. This is very important, and must not be skipped, neglected or bypassed.

> *If a man say, I love God, and hateth his brother, he is a liar: for he that loveth not his brother whom he hath seen, how can he love God whom he hath not seen? And this commandment have we from him, That he who loveth God love his brother also.*
>
> 1 John 4:20-21

If we do not love the brethren, then we have no relationship with God. John made it clear that *"God is love,"* and if God is in us, then we love one another. If the love for the brethren is not found in us, then neither is God.

When we are joined to the Beloved, we are joined to each other — like it or not. We are not given the choice of picking and choosing with whom we want to be connected. We're one family! There's an old saying, "You can pick your friends, but you can't pick your family."

In the family of God, there's no room for prejudice, preference or personality. Division of the family along lines of education, economic status, political persuasion, church denomination or ethnic origin isn't acceptable to God. If you have Jesus in your heart as Lord and Savior, you're a part of one family, in God, with His blood running in your veins.

Your relationship with the Beloved marries you to the Word. When you have a relationship with the Beloved and the Word, it marries you to the throne. You will not have any part of the throne if you refuse the relationship of the Beloved and the brethren (see 1 John 3,4). The world should know us because of the love we have one for another. It's sad, but there's often more gossip in the house of the Lord, concerning the brethren, than there is in the world, concerning friends. If Christ is the Head of the house, then He is capable of taking care of His children who are within His house.

Christians have a bad reputation of killing their own. If someone falls, we are quick to remind the fallen one of his sin, rather than picking him up, dusting him off, setting his feet on the right path, and then walking with him until he gets it right. We would rather gossip, behind closed doors, than to close the door of our own prayer closet and lift the sinner up before the Father.

When God looks at us, He doesn't look at who we

are, but at who we are to become — if we continue surrendering to Him. Isn't it about time that we give our brothers and sisters that same kind of love? We trash many individuals who have true callings and giftings because we can't see past who they are to who they will become. I'm sure that David's brothers, on the day he was anointed as king, looked and saw only their scrawny younger brother. On the day David went to take his brothers food, and heard Goliath challenging the army of Israel, he was filled with indignation. David's eldest brother was upset because of David's boldness. His brother couldn't, and didn't, want to see who was in front of him (1 Samuel 17:23-28).

Relationship deals with more than God and me, it encompasses the entire Church. We cannot walk in relationship with God and neglect the relationship of the Body.

The third aspect of relationship I want to discuss is that with the THRONE of God. We are being challenged to come face-to-face with God, who sits upon the throne. The chamber of intimacy is wonderful, but God does not stop there. He wants us to see Him in all of His fullness. When we come to the throne of God, we come face-to-face with the sovereignty of God, and our relationship changes beyond that of the chamber. The sovereignty of God is the attribute that establishes His rule over every creature, in Heaven and in Earth, and over the entire Universe. It is this attribute of God that makes Him a God whom we can depend on and trust. As a sovereign, He is absolutely independent. He always does as He pleases.

Declaring the end from the beginning, and from ancient times the things that are not yet done, saying, My counsel shall stand, and I WILL DO ALL MY PLEASURE. Isaiah 46:10

And all the inhabitants of the earth are reputed as nothing: and HE DOETH ACCORDING TO HIS WILL in the army of heaven, and among the inhabitants of the earth: and none can stay his hand, or say unto him, What doest thou? Daniel 4:35

When Jesus walked the Earth, He established God's Kingdom here in the hearts of men. He proclaimed the message of a holy kingdom and its established principles. We cannot find any place in Scripture where Jesus compromised or changed God's Kingdom principles to fit man's way of thinking or his lifestyle. God is sovereign. He is King, and as King, He rules with absolute authority.

The throne of God is the center of all things. It represents all authority, all power and all possession. It is the very birthplace of all of God's plans. It is the place where you find both His mercy and His judgements. It is the place from which all life flows and issues forth as a river:

And he shewed me a pure river of water of life, clear as crystal, proceeding out of the throne of God and of the Lamb. Revelation 22:1

It's important for us as members of the Church of the living God to understand the importance of His throne, as it has been established. God does not share His throne with anybody:

> *Who is like unto thee, O Lord, among the gods? who is like thee, glorious in holiness, fearful in praises, doing wonders?* Exodus 15:11

To walk in relationship with the throne of God is to understand the holiness of God and how He desires for us to be holy. If we cry out to know, and to walk with God, then we have to be willing to give up our own desires for His. If we want the mind of Christ, we must give up our own. The same is true with His heart.

Our mind is at enmity with God, unless it has been renewed by the Word. Our will, if not subjected to the will of God, will be in opposition to the things of God. There is nothing in you and me of any value, except God. Our intellect means nothing if it isn't wrapped in the knowledge of God. Our righteousness is filthy in the eyes of God. Once I have given my life to God, I give up the right to make my own decisions if I've given my life to God. Does this mean I am a puppet? No. But it does mean that I'm subject to my Lord, my Master and my King. It does mean that I want to please Him in every area of my life. It means that we are servants of the Most High God and subject to all of His desires. WOW! That's great!

True relationship is based on our ability to yield to God's plan for our lives. We bring ourselves into direct disobedience when we seek our own way, rather than His will for our lives. God does not want a kingdom full of puppets, but He does want obedient sons and daughters. If we're going to be a people of God's presence, then we will have to yield our entire lives over to Him. In His presence, we find life, and the richness of God.

The throne of God is a holy throne, and to walk in relationship means complete surrender and obedience. When the scripture states *"Be ye holy as I am holy,"* it isn't making a suggestion, it is giving a directive. It is requiring obedience. True relationship is found when we say yes to all that is pleasing to God.

SEVEN

GOING THE DISTANCE

And the Ancient of days did sit, whose garment was white as snow, and the hair of his head like the pure wool: his throne was like the fiery flame.

Daniel 7:9

Seeing a painting in an old museum of God sitting on His throne brought to my mind the living reality that God's presence truly flows in and through His temple. His presence, in our lives and in the life of the Church, isn't there only to bless us, empower us, heal us or ignite us — even though He does all that, and more. When God pours out His presence, it fills us, those who are the temple of His Spirit.

When we see and experience His presence, it's not enough just to stand in awe, but rather, it causes us to bow our knee in complete surrender and worship. When we surrender through faith, to His presence and His nature, then who He is becomes a part of who we are (see Ephesians 3:17-19). When we become like Him, we will truly become living epistles. Without Him, there is no life within us. Worship gives us the opportunity to see the Lord high and lifted up upon His throne. Our responsibility is to bow our knee in surrender to the authority of God.

Isaiah, upon seeing God's presence, worshiped Him. Worship led him to complete surrender, and surrender led him to the altar of God where one of the seraphim touched his lips with a coal from that altar. Thus, his life was changed forever.

Worship produces something in us, and it ministers to God. When we worship, we come face-to-face with the absolute authority of God, which is His throne. One cannot stand in the place of worship without bending the knee in surrender. I truly believe that we have not begun to scratch the surface of true worship. We have many expressions based in praise. However, there is a sound that's emerging from hearts that are crying out in complete surrender, as they behold Him face-to-face.

The longing to know God is a journey that carries us through great truths and deliverance. When Isaiah saw the train of God fill the temple, it changed His life forever. Looking at the picture presented by Isaiah's vision, the principal message of God's holiness is clear. However, there's another picture of holiness that may not be seen as easily. God wanted to use Isaiah, but He could not use him in his current condition. He had to be changed. Whenever God chooses to use man, He always sets him apart — this is holiness. In Exodus, priests were set apart (28:1); in Genesis, Abraham was called out (12:1); in 1 Samuel, David was separated (16:12-13) and Samuel the prophet was dedicated to the Lord (1:20, 27-28). God touched Isaiah's lips, separating him and cleansing his mouth for divine use. If we are God's temple, then we must be holy, for He cannot, and will not, reside in anything that isn't devoted totally to Him.

Scripture reveals that God no longer resides in temples made by the hands of men, but rather in the hearts of men. You and I are the temple of God (see 1 Corinthians 3:16 and 2 Corinthians 6:16). God wants to dwell in His temple — all of us. But if we try to lock Him in one room, we can't expect Him to stay. His desire is to come and enlarge Himself in us and live through us. He doesn't want us to live behind a veil of flesh. It was rent long ago, on Calvary, and we are to appropriate that truth into our lives:

> *For the time is come that judgment must begin at the house of God: and if it first begin at us, what shall the end be of them that obey not the gospel of God? And if the righteous scarcely be saved, where shall the ungodly and the sinner appear? Wherefore let them that suffer according to the will of God commit the keeping of their souls to him in well doing, as unto a faithful Creator.* 1 Peter 4:17-19

Judgement begins in the house of the Lord. God wants you and me to be His dwelling place. Whenever His presence is revealed, it's not to simply touch us, but to establish Himself in us. The application of judgement in the life of a believer is often disregarded and considered an Old Testament work. Repentance and judgement are based on who God is — His person. He is holy; therefore, anything that comes in contact with Him must be holy. Otherwise, He would cease to be holy, being contaminated by the profane.

When God revealed His Kingdom to John, the first thing he saw was not the sea of glass or the gates of pearl, but the throne:

> *And immediately I was in the spirit: and, behold, a throne was set in heaven, and one sat on the throne.*
>
> Revelation 4:2

The throne of God is established throughout all eternity. It is the center of all that God is. It is a holy throne. It is a throne that He desires to establish within you and me. To do so, He must come and judge the house. We think that because we live on this side of Calvary, we're excused from the work of judgement, but whenever God's presence begins to fill His temple, the work of sanctification always takes place.

Sanctification is a word that is seldom used today, because it denotes old-fashioned repentance. However, sanctification is a work that is directly related to the Word of God itself. It is the act of cleansing, through washing. The true work of sanctification is an operation by which the Holy Spirit applies the blood of Christ, and Jesus, who is the Word, comes and washes us clean. This is something we can't escape if we're going to allow the throne of God to be set up in our hearts.

Going the Distance

When I was young, my grandmother used to give me a "jaybird" bath. She would bring out a basin of water and put me in front of the furnace and quickly wash me so that I wouldn't get cold. Then there was the dreaded "spit" bath that my mother would give me before we walked into church or into a store. When it comes to the washing of sanctification, the hit-and-miss jaybird bath or the spit bath won't do. We have to be completely submerged in the truths of God.

God's presence, whenever revealed, begins the work of judgement in our lives. When we ask Him into our hearts, He comes in as Lord, King and Master. He wants to be the Lord over every area of our lives. He wants to be the complete authority. As our Master, there is no other to whom we should answer. We cannot walk as *People of His Presence* and serve two masters. The Scriptures tell us that a man who is double minded is *"unstable in all his ways"* (James 1:8).

In God, there is no place between the holy and the profane. Somehow, in our minds, there are shades of gray. There are areas that we excuse, overlook and ignore because we haven't looked at God's holiness as an absolute, unyielding factor that is a life-changing reality for our day. The children of Israel understood what holiness meant. They watched as God consumed Aaron's sons for not having offered holy fire. They knew the instructions concerning God's holy Temple, and kept them, knowing that the alternative held stern consequences.

Unfortunately, today we don't esteem the house of God or the things of God as holy. We often treat them with a casual appreciation, seldom reverencing Him or

His house as a place of holiness. We come in late, skip out early, miss when it suits our activities, give only what's expected, complain when asked for more, and keep the Word of God by our beds as nighttime reading material (and if we open it, we soon sleep). We expect God to be on time (without fail), to give to us abundantly, to never leave us, and to fill us with new revelation. I don't mean for this to sound harsh, but we're living in a time in which the world is looking to the Church for signs of life, conviction, truth, integrity, commitment and covenant. Will the world find what it's looking for?

In the days of old, God's Temple was a place of sacrifice, cleansing, service and worship. Even though the temple of our hearts is not made by hands, the same truths hold fast. We, as the temple of the living God, are to offer our lives as living sacrifices:

> *I beseech you therefore, brethren, by the mercies of God, that ye present your bodies a living sacrifice, holy, acceptable unto God, which is your reasonable service.* Romans 12:1

God calls us to live daily as holy sacrifices, acceptable to Him. The sacrifice of our lives is not something that's done once a year, as were the sacrifices of burnt offerings in the days of old. Our sacrifice to the Father is to be presented continually. When you and I take up the cross daily, we become a picture of forgiveness, restoration and deliverance to the entire world. Paul wrote:

> *We are troubled on every side, yet not distressed; we are perplexed, but not in despair; persecuted, but not*

forsaken; cast down, but not destroyed; always bearing about in the body the dying of the Lord Jesus, that the life also of Jesus might be made manifest in our body. For we which live are alway delivered unto death for Jesus' sake, that the life also of Jesus might be made manifest in our mortal flesh. So then death worketh in us, but life in you. 2 Corinthians 4:8-12

For our light affliction, which is but for a moment, worketh for us a far more exceeding and eternal weight of glory. 2 Corinthians 4:17

When you received Jesus into your heart, it was not a free ticket to an easy and smooth life. Indeed, the contrary is true. It was an open invitation for affliction, persecution, trials and distress. The Great Shepherd knows that shearing is not an easy process, but He also knows that it is necessary. If sheep aren't continually sheared, they get heavy and become easy targets for their predators, or are easily smitten by the forces of nature. In Australia and New Zealand, where herding sheep is a primary source of income, shepherds know that if they don't maintain their flocks, a heavy torrential rainfall could cause the sheep's wool to become saturated and very heavy, causing them to fall over and drown in their own wool.

The same is true of us. If we are not sheared, we become heavy in pride and in self-importance, overly reliant upon self. Lack of spiritual shearing is dangerous to the life of a believer. Sheep need shearing, and our Shepherd wants our fleece. We only need to decide to go to Him without a word, not kicking and screaming. Lambs go without a sound.

How you surrender to shearing is important. It can make a world of difference, since shearing isn't always easy. If you buck against the cutters, you could emerge all nicked up. But if you allow the controlled hands of God to come upon you, be sure He knows exactly how and what to do. We have this assurance — though we may be troubled, perplexed, afflicted, persecuted and cast down — that we will never be forsaken. God uses many things in our lives to shear us. It's a process we cannot escape. And we must have confidence that we're never alone and never mishandled by God.

God is a fire, but He is a controlled fire. You do not have to fear the flames:

> *The voice of the LORD divideth the flames of fire.*
> Psalm 29:7

We can trust the fire, for He knows how to divide the flames. Affliction is only for a moment, but the eternal weight of glory that it produces is what brings us into mature relationship.

Our journey may be difficult, steep and rocky, but the treasure we find is worth going the distance. As Paul wrote:

> *I press toward the mark for the prize of the high calling of God in Christ Jesus.* Philippians 3:14

To *press* is to "act with steadily applied weight, or force; to hold close, as in an embrace." My children and

Going the Distance

I have a little saying we tell each other when I'm out of town: "I eat you up; I love you so." God is waiting to hear the same from you and me. He wants us to hold Him so tight that it hurts. When we do, He will truly be a part of us, and we can say with boldness:

> *For in him we live, and move, and have our being.*
>
> Acts 17:28

EIGHT

THE SEARCHING HEART

By night on my bed I sought him whom my soul loveth: I sought him, but I found him not. I will rise now, and go about the city in the streets, and in the broad ways I will seek him whom my soul loveth: I sought him, but I found him not. The watchmen that go about the city found me: to whom I said, Saw ye him whom my soul loveth? It was but a little that I passed from them, but I found him whom my soul loveth: I held him, and would not let him go, until I had brought him into my mother's house, and into the chamber of her that conceived me.

Song of Solomon 3:1-4

As mentioned in Chapter Four, the longing to know God is placed deep within the heart of man. It is a longing that is stirred by the hand of God, causing us to seek Him diligently until we find Him. Here, in the Song of

Solomon, we have a wonderful picture of the searching heart.

All too often we begin our search for God in the place of comfort, or familiarity: *"By night on my bed I sought him whom my soul loveth."* The place of comfort is generally where we are stirred, but seldom is it the place where we find Him. Comfort is not always from God. Often, the opposite is true. Comfort is a place of ease. Growth comes through stretching, and character is developed through trial. There are times when God allows us some breathing room, but these times are seldom long, and they are never permanent. When we're stirred, we're moved to action. When we're comfortable, we're at ease. Paul warned:

> *But ye, brethren, are not in darkness, that that day should overtake you as a thief. Ye are all the children of light, and the children of the day: we are not of the night, nor of darkness. Therefore let us not sleep, as do others; but let us watch and be sober. For they that sleep sleep in the night; and they that be drunken are drunken in the night. But let us, who are of the day, be sober, putting on the breastplate of faith and love; and for an helmet, the hope of salvation.*
>
> 1 Thessalonians 5:4-8

If we are to find Him whom our souls long for, we must rise: *"I will rise now..."* You will never find Him unless you pursue Him. He doesn't run from us, but He makes finding Him worth the journey.

The second place that we tend to look for Him is in the place of business: *"and go about the streets..."* But business and activity do not necessarily mean we will find the One we long for. Business can be just that — busy-ness. There are times we get so caught up in activity that we don't realize the cloud of His presence has moved.

Another place that one may look to find Him is in the *"broad ways,"* or areas that are popular. Popularity is an area where we have to be very careful. Just because a place is popular doesn't mean it's right for you. Generally, a popular place is comfortable and accepted. Popularity isn't being elite, as the world would have you believe. Rather, it's going along with whatever happens to be.

As parents, it's vital for you to stress the pitfalls of popularity to your young people. To be popular means to go along with the "in thing," and the "in thing" is usually the wrong thing.

Soon, the woman presented in Solomon's song finds that the one her soul loves isn't in the city or in the broad way: *"I sought him, but I found him not."* Unsuccessful in her pursuit, she asked the watchmen, who had found her, if they knew where her beloved was. I believe that this is one of the saddest illustrations of leadership found in the Scriptures. The watchmen were not where they were supposed to be, on the wall. It's imperative that you be where God has planted you. The journey to find God will never take you away from responsibility. You cannot neglect your responsibility if you expect to hold on to a clear vision and have lucid insight. Revelation comes when you are obedient to God's instructions. If you're in leadership, stay faithful to the task that God has called you to. Don't neglect the purpose of God in your life. Maintain your relationship daily, so that you can point others to the One they are seeking.

The woman of Solomon's song went just a little ways past the watchmen, and there she found her beloved. *"It was but a little that I passed from them, but I found him whom my soul loveth: I held him, and would not let him go, until I had brought him into my mother's house, and into the chamber of her that conceived me."* When we find the One whom our souls long for, what do we do? Jacob, when He wrestled with the Lord, said, *"I will not let thee go, except thou bless me"* (Genesis 32:26). How determined are we to find God? And when we find Him, how determined are we to see Him?

Finding our Beloved is but the first step. We need to be ready to take Him home: *"I brought him into my mothers house."* When we invite Him, we should be willing for Him to come in, all the way. We cannot withhold anything from Him. He doesn't want to put just one foot inside of our door, and we can't cut Him up, taking the parts we like. We have to receive Him in His totality.

When she found him, she not only took him home, but she also took him into her mother's bedchamber. When we find Him, He wants to touch every part of our lives, and often there are areas in our past that we don't easily give up. We want to keep our disappointments, our unforgiveness, our bitterness, our insecurities and our failures. But it's useless to seek God if we aren't willing to receive Him in His fullness. When we see Him in His fullness, He penetrates our deepest sorrows and our darkest fears. In seeing Him, we become like Him.

To be a *People of His Presence* we must commit ourselves to Him completely. There is a longing to be with Him. There is a journey to His throne. And most assuredly, there is a revelation of His holiness.

Nine

A Polished Shaft

And he hath made my mouth like a sharp sword; in the shadow of his hand hath he hid me, and made me a polished shaft; in his quiver hath he hid me; and said unto me, Thou art my servant, O Israel, in whom I will be glorified. Isaiah 49:2-3

This is a wonderful picture of God's preparation in our lives, and of the journey that one of God's servants endured. During Isaiah's vision of God's throne, one of the seraphim came and touched his mouth with a coal from the altar of God, to cleanse his lips. Then he heard the voice of God asking, *"Whom shall I send, and who will go for us?"* Isaiah responded, *"Here am I; send me."* From that moment on, he was a man with scarred lips. But what the Lord told him next would have to have been alarming. People would hear him, but they would not understand. They would see, but not perceive. In other words, the call that Isaiah had just answered wasn't going to be easy to fulfill. He would be misunderstood and rejected and would see few results.

How would we like to enter a ministry having been told that our message would be ineffectual? The announcement might sound something like this: "Wanted, anyone who will go in the name of the Lord, suffer persecution and be misunderstood and rejected." That's exactly the commission we have been given:

> *Beloved, think it not strange concerning the fiery trial which is to try you, as though some strange thing happened unto you: but rejoice, inasmuch as ye are partakers of Christ's sufferings; that, when his glory shall be revealed, ye may be glad also with exceeding joy. If ye be reproached for the name of Christ, happy are ye; for the spirit of glory and of God resteth upon you: on their part he is evil spoken of, but on your part he is glorified.* 1 Peter 4:12-14

Isaiah's mouth became a sharp sword. His words went right to the point. He was deliberate and spoke with accuracy, and God used him to speak of the coming salvation. We should note that our own words, when we speak the Gospel, are to be tempered and salted with grace; otherwise they will be so sharp that they'll be destructive.

God made Isaiah into a polished shaft. In the making of a polished shaft, many things take place. First, the skilled craftsman picks a branch from a tree. This may be compared to the way God picks His instruments.

A Polished Shaft

And we know that all things work together for good to them that love God, to them who are the called according to his purpose. For whom he did foreknow, he also did predestinate to be conformed to the image of his Son, that he might be the firstborn among many brethren. Moreover whom he did predestinate, them he also called: and whom he called, them he also justified: and whom he justified, them he also glorified.

Romans 8:28-30

As a craftsman who picks a branch, without looking closely at what it is, but at what it will become, God also picks us. He is not really concerned with what we presently are, but He looks at what He can make of us if we surrender to Him and to His dealing and preparation.

After the craftsman picks the branch, he begins to pull off its beautiful foliage. God does the same, and when we come before Him, He starts stripping our "foliage" — our trophies, our titles and our abilities. He wants us to stand naked, as we truly are, before Him.

Several months ago, while attending a women's conference, I heard the Spirit of the Lord speak to me concerning His stripping. He said, "I desire a stripped lover." He further told me that He wanted a lover who was willing to allow the lights to be turned on so that He could see everything. When we come to Him and hide any part of ourselves from His view, we're saying to Him, "I don't trust You."

But God, our Beloved, will never handle us improperly. He won't laugh at our imperfections, or make us feel uncomfortable or insecure.

God went on to show me that an intimate relationship isn't possible without nakedness. A fully clothed relationship is based on pretending and imagination. The Scriptures reveal that the imagination of men is evil:

> *Then said he unto me, Son of man, hast thou seen what the ancients of the house of Israel do in the dark, every man in the chambers of his imagery? for they say, The LORD seeth us not; the LORD hath forsaken the earth. He said also unto me, Turn thee yet again, and thou shalt see greater abominations that they do.*
>
> Ezekiel 8:12-13

When we come to God, He wants us to come to Him in truth, not pretending, but in honesty and uprightness. A naked relationship unmasks the imagination, but those who only strip from the waist down seek self-gratification and individual pleasure. If we desire true intimacy, we must be willing to strip ourselves of all distractions, of all time restraints, and of all our coverings.

When David brought in the ark of God's presence, he stripped himself of his kingly robes. When the King of kings comes to us, we would do well to realize that our fleshly covering is of no importance, and that keeping it, or part of it, will only impair our relationship.

God strips us of any foliage that would keep Him from seeing us as we really are. After all the leaves are removed, only a crooked, knobby, little branch is left. It's not very attractive, but the Master Craftsman is not interested in its outward appearance. He's looking on the inside.

A Polished Shaft

God told Samuel — on the day he went to anoint the next king of Israel from the house of Jesse — not to look on outward appearances, but on the heart. David, of his father's entire household, was the least likely candidate. His own father didn't even bother to call him from the field to stand before the prophet.

God never looks at us in the way man does. Man looks at pedigree, economic status, gender and education. It is unfortunate that the church also judges a man by these same attributes, rather than looking to see if the heart of the person is surrendered to God. Anointing and authority have absolutely nothing to do with our outward achievements.

After the foliage has been stripped away, the craftsman takes the branch and plunges it into water. He knows that by allowing the water to be absorbed into the fibers of the branch, it will become pliable. If this were not done, the branch would snap and break under the pressure of his work. God wants us to be pliable in His hands. He wants us to bend when the winds blow, and not snap and break.

Several years ago, we went through Hurricane Hugo. By the time the great storm made landfall, it was night. I remember that when we opened the door the next morning, devastation was visible everywhere. Houses had been blown off their foundations, boats were in people's yards, and telephone poles were lying across the streets like pick up sticks. But what stood out the most were the trees. Everywhere you looked, trees were down and had been snapped in two. Some were pushed right through people's houses, and some you couldn't even find. Only a hole was left where they had been uprooted. Only the tall, skinny trees with deep roots seemed to have survived. They were able to bend and sway with the wind.

When we allow the water of the Word to flow into our lives, it will keep us pliable in God's hands. Without the water of the Word, we snap and break every time the wind changes direction.

Once the water was locked into every fiber of the branch, the craftsman could lift the soggy limb out of the water and place it within a vise. This vise would serve to straighten out any crooks and bends. To be God's instrument, we will be straightened, and become single-minded. The Scriptures declare: *"A double minded man is unstable in all his ways"* (James 1:8). When it comes to God, our own opinion is of no importance. It's one too many. When we are single-minded, we have but one thought, and that is to please the Father and to do His will.

Jesus was the greatest example of this. He never did anything outside the will of the Father. He told those who followed Him that He did only what He saw His Father in Heaven doing. In Scripture, there's a theme that concerns the singular quality of God. Great importance is placed on having singleness of vision, which is called *"doves' eyes"* (Song of Solomon 1:15) and *"singleness of heart"* (Ephesians 6:5).

Every day the craftsman would check the branch and tighten the vise. In the same way, God is constantly checking and directing. The enemy can't do anything if the Father doesn't allow it. God Himself tightens the vise.

He alone knows how much pressure to add. He controls the winds that blow, the seas that rage and the waters that rise. Everything He permits is especially designed with a purpose in mind. He knows where He's taking us and what He wants us to become, so that He can shoot us forth as perfect polished shafts that will go directly to the work He has sent us. We must trust Him.

When the branch emerges, it's perfectly straight. Any wayward tendencies have been worked out, and it stands straight and tall.

Next, it is rubbed down with oil. Oil has special properties. It is used in several ways: for gladness, for separation, for sacrifice, and for consecration. The craftsman knows that the oil will seal in all of the properties that have been worked into the shaft. Without oil in our lives, we have no sign of separation, anointing or authority.

The oil that was used for anointing was a specific kind. It had to be pure olive oil (Exodus 25:6, 27:20 and 35:14). Jesus fulfilled the meaning of the symbol provided by that oil when He was beaten and pressed in the garden of Gethsemane. The name *Gethsemane* means "olive press."

The work of applying the oil is the work of the Holy Spirit. He applies the finished work of Christ to our lives. Christ is the Anointed One, and we are anointed as we allow Him to be added to our lives.

After the shaft is anointed, it is polished and buffed. For us, this process is very uncomfortable. God often uses those who are closest to us to buff our lives. The Scriptures remind us that we are lively stones, crowded together. If we look at certain gems in their raw state, we see ugly rocks, but when thrown into a tumbler, these ugly rocks emerge with brilliance and gain value.

While the shaft has been going through these various stages, the craftsman has been busy fashioning its tip. Once the shaft has been soaked, dried, pressed, oiled and buffed, it's ready for the tip to be applied. This represents our mandate, or commission. God has commissioned each of us to a specific task.

When we receive our tip, our anointing, we often think we're ready for ministry. However, this is actually the time when we are the most dangerous. We need for God to place us within His quiver: *"He made me a polished shaft; in his quiver hath he hid me."* For many of us, this is the most difficult stage of the process. We've been picked, stripped, washed, anointed, buffed, given our mandate, and now we must be hid! I'll never forget when I was going through this difficult stage. It wasn't easy. It may have been the most frustrating time of my life. I felt like a soda that had been shaken, but the cap was still in place, and I was full of pressure and just fizzing. God knew that if He released me, I would make a mess.

I was like a racehorse, kicking against the stall, wanting to get out on the track. One day, Dr. Baker told me I could keep kicking all I wanted, but the only thing I was going to do was hurt my foot. The walls of the stall wouldn't be taken down until they had accomplished their purpose.

Finally, in frustration, I asked the Father to show me the season of my preparation, and in His mercy He showed me a picture of myself standing under a giant leaf. I was entirely covered, except for the tip of my nose, which was the only part of me in the sunlight. From that moment on, I didn't struggle against the stall, and I didn't ask to be removed from the quiver. I realized that it was the quiver that would take the "I" out of "glorified."

> *In his quiver hath he hid me; and said unto me, Thou art my servant, O Israel, in whom I will be glorified.*

If we are still important to ourselves, we cannot glorify God. "I," our ego, can't be allowed into "glorified." God's purpose isn't about "I." It's about glorifying God. And for this to happen, we have to come to the place that we lose our own identity. The only identity that we need is to be found in God. Titles and accomplishments are not important. We only need to know who we are in God. Once we become secure in that knowledge, we can walk boldly in our convictions.

The journey is never easy, but it's necessary. If we are to be a *People of His Presence* we must not be concerned with what His presence can do for us, or through us, but rather, what His presence will do in us. When we reach this point of maturity, God's presence is first, and foremost, in our lives. Once He has shown Himself *to* us, then, and only then, He can shine *through* us.

Once our time in the quiver is accomplished, we emerge, but having God's plan and not our own. Then He can shoot us forth, and we will hit our mark with accuracy. If we had been shot prematurely, we would have fallen short of the mark, and the preparation and the journey would have been in vain.

If you allow God to take you through every step, He won't leave you, nor will He neglect you, but He will stretch you and perfectly prepare you.

Ten

The Treasure Within

For God, who commanded the light to shine out of darkness, hath shined in our hearts, to give the light of the knowledge of the glory of God in the face of Jesus Christ. But we have this treasure in earthen vessels, that the excellency of the power may be of God, and not of us. 2 Corinthians 4:6-7

The journey toward being a *People of His Presence* is often full of obstacles. These obstacles do not have the purpose of deterring us, but are placed before us to work in us God's eternal purposes. Once we conquer each obstacle, we are one step closer to the likeness of Christ.

Several years ago I pondered a common phrase. We say, "God gave me a revelation," or "I heard a fresh revelation." Generally, we understand that a revelation is something that becomes known to us supernaturally, something that we didn't know before. But when I began to look at this subject a little more closely, I discovered that a revelation isn't only something that we see, or come to know, but it's also something that is to be worked in us. When God reveals Himself or His Word, it's not simply to give us knowledge for knowledge's sake. His purpose is for us to become like what He has revealed. As Paul wrote to the Corinthians:

> *But we all, with open face beholding as in a glass the glory of the Lord, are changed into the same image from glory to glory, even as by the Spirit of the LORD.*
>
> 2 Corinthians 3:18

When we look in the mirror and see the glory of the Lord, the revelation isn't given to us so that we can merely behold Him, but rather so that we can become like Him. We are only earthen vessels, but when the glory of the Lord is revealed to us, and worked in us, we have this hope, *"which is Christ in you, the hope of glory"* (Colossians 1:27). To Timothy, Paul wrote:

> *But in a great house there are not only vessels of gold and of silver, but also of wood and of earth; and some to honour, and some to dishonour. If a man therefore purge himself from these, he shall be a vessel unto honour, sanctified, and meet for the master's use, and prepared unto every good work.*
>
> 2 Timothy 2:20-21

In today's society that's so value conscious, we might read this portion and conclude that the value of the vessels mentioned by Paul lay in the material of which they were made: gold, silver, wood and earth. We would conclude that gold is the most costly. However, when you look closely, the value is in the honor, and the lack of value in the dishonor. The treasure is not the outward appearance, but it's what lies inside:

> *For God, who commanded the light to shine out of darkness, hath shined in our hearts, to give the light of the knowledge of the glory of God in the face of Jesus Christ. But we have this treasure in earthen vessels, that the excellency of the power may be of God, and not of us.* 2 Corinthians 4:6-7

Throughout the Word of God, there is a thread that points out the creative aspect of God. In Genesis, He is the Creator; in Ezra, He is the Master Builder; in Ezekiel, He is the Promised Restorer; in Amos, He is the Plumb Line; in James, He is Our Healer. God has the ability to create and to re-create.

Jeremiah gave a great illustration of this. He pointed out the living truth that God is the Potter and His people are clay. Each of us, then, is but a lump of dirt, waiting to be molded into a vessel fit for the Master's use.

In the beginning, man was fashioned out of *"the dust of the ground"*:

> *And the LORD God formed man of the dust of the ground, and breathed into his nostrils the breath of life; and man became a living soul.* Genesis 2:7

Dirt cannot become clay unless water is present. Water gives it the moldable and pliable quality that makes it clay. With this in mind, could it be that God the Father took of the earth, Jesus the Son (the Word) provided the water, the Holy Spirit (the *Ruach*) gave the breath of life, and together the triune Godhead created man? After all, the Scriptures state *"after OUR image, after OUR likeness."*

When we consider this, it brings together a picture of how we can reveal the complete work of the glory of God. The triune Godhead is a truth that is often hard to conceive: three separate entities, yet one God. They do not function independently, but have different functions. We walk in the truths of each one, yet they reveal the same truth. This is something that we have to accept in faith. It isn't something that is easily understood. It can't even be explained by profound intellectual theory and calculation. But then again, it's not supposed to be.

In the beginning, when man was fashioned after the image of the Godhead, he walked as the express image of the Divine. When man fell, a veil of flesh was formed, and a death occurred. Man no longer walked as the glorious image of God, but now in the state of a fallen man.

Thank God that through Christ we can be restored to God's image. It requires a process of transformation:

> *But we all, with open face beholding as in a glass the glory of the Lord, are changed into the same image from glory to glory, even as by the Spirit of the Lord.*
> 2 Corinthians 3:18

Let us look carefully at the process of transformation:

> *The word which came to Jeremiah from the LORD, saying, Arise, and go down to the potter's house, and there I will cause thee to hear my words. Then I went down to the potter's house, and, behold, he wrought a work on the wheels. And the vessel that he made of clay was marred in the hand of the potter: so he made it again another vessel, as seemed good to the potter to make it. Then the word of the LORD came to me, saying, O house of Israel,* CANNOT I DO WITH YOU AS THIS POTTER? *saith the LORD. Behold, as the clay is in the potter's hand, so are ye in mine hand, O house of Israel. At what instant I shall speak concerning a nation, and concerning a kingdom, to pluck up, and to pull down, and to destroy it; if that nation, against whom I have pronounced, turn from their evil, I will repent of the evil that I thought to do unto them. And at what instant I shall speak concerning a nation, and concerning a kingdom, to build and to plant it; if it do evil in my sight, that it obey not my voice, then I will repent of the good, wherewith I said I would benefit them.* Jeremiah 18:1-10

Remember, God is the Potter, and because He is the Potter, it's not up to us to question His decisions. As Paul wrote to the Roman believers:

> *Nay but, O man, who art thou that repliest against God? Shall the thing formed say to him that formed it, Why hast thou made me thus? Hath not the potter power over the clay; of the same lump to make one vessel unto honour, and another unto dishonour?*

> *What if God, willing to shew his wrath, and to make his power known, endured with much longsuffering the vessels of wrath fitted to destruction: and that he might make known the riches of his glory on the vessels of mercy, which he had afore prepared unto glory, even us, whom he hath called, not of the Jews only, but also of the Gentiles?* Romans 9:20-24

It's not up to us, mere lumps of clay, to decide, or dictate, what we want. God, the Potter, knows what He has need of and makes the vessel accordingly. Our only responsibility is to stay pliable to His touch.

In the same way that many limbs and parts make up the human body, each believer has a specific place or function within the Body of Christ. The Father places each of us according to our particular grace (see Romans 12:6, Ephesians 4:8-12, and 2 Timothy 1:9-11).

God spoke to Jeremiah and told him to arise and go down to the potter's house so that he could hear His words. It is interesting to note that God tells Jeremiah to *"go down"* to the potter's house. Often, transformation comes about in the low places. The Jordan River, the place between God's promise and the Promised Land, was a place of sudden descent. If you are waiting on a fulfillment from God, you can rest assured it won't come until you're brought to a place of sudden descent.

God told Joshua, at the Jordan:

> *Sanctify yourselves: for to morrow the* LORD *will do wonders among you.* Joshua 3:5

Without sanctification you won't be able to enter into the fulfilled word of the Lord. God will see to it that you are cleansed, since cleansing determines the honor or dishonor of a vessel.

When Jeremiah entered the house, he saw that the potter was making a vessel upon the wheel. Suddenly the potter marred the vessel. There are many reasons why a potter might disfigure a vessel. The potter might feel that a foreign substance, such as a rock or a stick, was in the clay, and he knows if this foreign material remains, when the vessel comes to the firing process, the heat will cause the vessel to crack.

The potter may feel that there's too much air within the clay. In that case, he may take the clay back into his hand, and with great pressure, knead the clay until the air is removed. The potter knows that if air is present, the vessel will pop or even explode in the furnace. It will require intense heat for the clay to become a fine vessel and the potter wants the vessel to endure, so he carefully removes any substance that could cause it to collapse in the furnace.

One of the most important reasons that will cause a potter to mar the clay is if he feels resistance. The process of forming a vessel isn't quick, and the clay must be able to endure the entire process. The potter knows how to knead the clay until all of its resistance is worked out. He is careful to keep adding water, to ensure the clay's flexibility.

Once Jeremiah saw the potter mar the vessel, the Lord asked a very important question, *"CANNOT I DO WITH YOU AS THIS POTTER?"* That is a serious question! Not only was He asking if Israel could be molded, but He was asking if they were willing to risk being marked as needing further processing. This is a decision that we're all faced with at one time or another. If necessary, are we willing to be made all over again? Are we willing to be placed on the wheel one more time?

The wheel that a potter uses is interesting. It's called a "throwing wheel," and it is kept moving by a kick plate. Because the potter never takes his hands off of the clay, he uses his foot to kick a long board attached to the bottom of a table.

The function of the wheel is to keep the clay in motion. This can be difficult, even overwhelming, but it's absolutely necessary. If the clay doesn't keep moving, the vessel being formed will end up lopsided, and won't be equally proportioned. God knows when to place us on the wheel, how fast to spin, and when to stop spinning.

The potter uses the throwing wheel to make meticulous adjustments throughout the process of transformation. There are certain times in each of our lives that we feel the spinning and the "throwing." In the same manner that the potter uses the kick plate to keep the clay in motion, our Potter knows how to use life's circumstances to keep us moving toward Him.

The Potter knows how to use the perfect combination of water, pressure and spinning to bring forth balanced results. We can trust His touch. It is never too soft or too hard. He is deliberate in all His actions. He never places us on the wheel just to watch us spin. We could say that He never causes us to lose time, just spinning our wheels. He always has a definite purpose and objective.

When the potter finishes spinning the vessel, and it has reached its final form, it's ready for the drying process and then the firing. This can also be a painful time in the life of the believer who doesn't rest in the fact that Jesus is the fourth man in the fire. God's fire has many purposes. It solidifies the clay in its current form.

The potter knows that the fire is hot, and he knows that the fire may be destructive if the clay doesn't surrender to the elevated temperature. When the fire has accomplished its task, a vessel will emerge, fit for the master's use.

There is one final process in the life of a fine vessel that I wish to cover. It is repair and cleaning. Once a vessel has gone through each and every process and is placed in function, several things may take place. Because of constant use, it could become weakened and need repair. Perhaps the vessel has been dropped or mishandled, causing it to chip or crack. Maybe, because of constant emptying, the vessel's mouth, or lip, has widened. A vessel in need of repair can become ineffective in its function if it is not maintained.

A potter can repair a weakened vessel in one of several ways. First, he will empty it and remove any buildup or residue.

Our Potter knows that even though it is a painful process, the old residue must be removed so that it will not affect the treasured contents. We must occasionally allow ourselves to be emptied into the hands of the Potter so that He can fill us again.

I've often thought of people in terms of a pair of black pants. This is strange, I know, but every time I wear a pair of black pants (especially linen) they pick up everything. Every speck of lint shows. When our Potter empties us, everything must go. Everything that we have waited for, worked for, and achieved is poured out, reminding us that it's all about Him. No one escapes this process. Pain, hurt and rejection often become faithful companions to those who don't know how to lay themselves at God's feet. These "friends" will not only become a part of your life, but they'll be molded into your character if God isn't allowed to come in and scrape out the scum they have formed.

There is a saying: I will forgive you, but I'll never forget. This attitude isn't godly. These words should never be heard in the Church. When you choose to hold on to your hurts, you give them ground where they can take root. Once they take root, they will produce jealousy, bitterness, discord, strife and rebellion — some of the more notorious results of unforgiveness. Remember that when someone hurts you, if you'll quickly give God the pain, He will turn your pain into victory.

Vessels that have been dropped or mishandled, especially over a long period of time, may develop chips, nicks and cracks. If these aren't smoothed, they'll catch and scratch anyone who comes in contact with them. To restore the vessel, the potter will carefully sand and scrape the rough edges until all signs of abuse are gone.

Several years ago, I went through a series of great hurts. For months I withdrew from everyone, convinced that I was not withdrawing, but getting alone with God. I became careful not to get too close, or too personal with others. I carried on with business as usual, but in my attempt to handle the situation myself, I became abrasive. My hurts were catching on to everything and everybody, until one day when I walked into church with a smile plastered on my face, and one of the members grabbed me and wouldn't let me go. I tried everything. I stiffened up, hoping she would get the hint, but she detained me. I took a step backwards, thinking she would notice that I was making a point, but she held on. The longer she held me, the fuller I became, until all of a sudden the dam broke.

I learned through this that withdrawing to hide from any situation means that I have not given my hurts to God. You cannot go underground and stay guarded and protective if you want to be healed.

Jesus came as a clay vessel when He came as the Son of Man, but within Him was the treasure and the truth of the Son of God. Who He was had nothing to do with His outward appearance. Isaiah said of Him:

> *He hath no form nor comeliness; and when we shall see him, there is no beauty that we should desire him.*
>
> Isaiah 53:2

Who Jesus was had everything to do with the Father. He came as clay and was rejected, bruised, and broken. He was poured out long before He was nailed to the tree. The issue isn't what we are, since we are merely clay, but who we are, because God abides in us. Our clay packaging means nothing to God. He doesn't care about gender, color or status. The only thing He cares about is our hearts.

I believe God is asking us the same question He asked Jeremiah: *"Cannot I do with you as this potter?"* Many of His vessels need to be put back on the potter's wheel and reworked. God's question is not easy to answer, but it's a question that holds eternal value. Allow God to make you into a vessel of honor, fit for the Master's use.

ELEVEN

ABIDING, THE KEY TO RELATIONSHIP

May Christ through your faith [actually] dwell (settle down, abide, make His permanent home) in your hearts! May you be rooted deep in love and founded securely on love, that you may have the power and be strong to apprehend and grasp with all the saints [God's devoted people, the experience of that love] what is the breadth and length and height and depth [of it]; [that you really come] to know [practically, through experience for yourselves] the love of Christ, which far surpasses mere knowledge [without experience]; that you may be filled [through all your being] unto all the fullness of God [may have the richest measure of the divine Presence, and become a body wholly filled and flooded with God Himself]!

Ephesians 3:17-19, Amplified

When Christ abides in you through faith, you become a foundation upon which God can expand Himself. This passage from Ephesians explains that when God makes His permanent dwelling within you, you have the ability to know, beyond mere knowledge, the fullness of God. The relationship of abiding is more than knowledge, for knowledge by itself is empty of all life and value — unless it is tested. I'm always telling my congregation that knowledge, without trial and testing, is simply information, but when the knowledge you have is tried, then, and only then, can it become a part of who you are.

I could go my entire life knowing someone by name, and that person could still be a stranger to me. If I am not willing to put forth the effort, spending time with the individual and getting to know who the person is, that one will be no different to me than someone I pass on the street. There would be only one small difference; I would have a partial truth concerning the person: his or her name. Churches are full of people who walk in partial truths. Often, they only have a portion of God, and yet they build platforms of preference for their own doctrines, according to their own likes and dislikes.

It doesn't have to be that way. Abiding in Christ is something that can be done anywhere in the world. It reaches all across the globe, from the bushman in a poverty-stricken area of the world, to a businessman on Wall Street. Both of these individuals, in Christ, become our brothers.

Abiding is the first step to a true relationship, and the ultimate step to God's presence. Without it, there is no foundation upon which God can openly reveal Himself.

When you are committed to abiding in Him, you submit yourself wholly to Him. He then can enlarge you with the fullness and richness of His very nature.

God is ever-revealing, like a perfectly-cut diamond, which shows its beauty in its many facets (the polished or cut planes of the gem's surface). Each facet reveals color, light and texture. Together, they form a rich splendor. God isn't a flat God. He has many aspects, and each one complements the other. Throughout all eternity the angels will never grow tired of proclaiming Holy! Holy! Holy! as they look upon His unfolding beauty.

Each of God's attributes, emotions and directions reveals the fullness of His character. God is not a distant God. He wishes to unfold His nature within each of us. In this way, we can walk as living epistles, proclaiming the fullness of the Father.

He is calling us to deeper depths and higher heights in our relationship with Him. It isn't sufficient to walk in knowledge, simply for the sake of knowing. There are two kinds of knowledge. One is mental acknowledgment. This knowledge is based on what one has read, studied, observed or learned. The other is knowledge that is based on experience. It is what you have tasted, felt and seen. Anyone who has looked for a job right out of school knows the difference between these two classes of knowledge, having been found unqualified for many openings because of a lack of experience.

One of the best ways to understand the idea of head knowledge versus experiential knowledge is to look at the relationship between a young man and a young woman. In our society, a man and a woman go through the social custom of dating. They enjoy various activities with each other, which allow them to get to know each other. This knowledge establishes the foundation upon which they decide whether or not to pursue a future together.

If they decide to pursue the relationship further, they will go through an engagement period. This allows the couple to progress in their understanding of each other. Their conversations now become more intimate and detailed. This is a wonderful time of growth.

Soon, if all goes well, the couple will become dissatisfied with this limited relationship and long for greater intimacy. Words are wonderful, but they're so superficial when seen in the light of intimacy. Once the couple has been united as man and wife, they will be joined and become one flesh. Everything they have learned up until that point will become sealed in their hearts and lives. Their head knowledge of each other, which has carried them to this point, will be engulfed by their intimacy. From that day forward, everything they come to know will be filtered through their experiential intimacy.

Knowledge of God is the beginning, but this knowledge must grow until you become engulfed in intimacy with the Beloved. Spending time in worship, in prayer, and in the Word of God joins you with the heart of God. In His abiding intimacy, one comes to know His breadth, height and depth.

Jesus spoke to His disciples concerning the principle of abiding:

Abiding, the Key to Relationship

I am the true vine, and my Father is the husbandman. Every branch in me that beareth not fruit he taketh away: and every branch that beareth fruit, he purgeth it, that it may bring forth more fruit. Now ye are clean through the word which I have spoken unto you. Abide in me, and I in you. As the branch cannot bear fruit of itself, except it abide in the vine; no more can ye, except ye abide in me. I am the vine, ye are the branches: He that abideth in me, and I in him, the same bringeth forth much fruit: for without me ye can do nothing. John 15:1-5

Jesus said that unless we abide in Him, and He in us, we cannot bear, or produce, any fruit. A branch cannot survive without the vine to which it is connected. The vine is its source of life. Once the Church becomes completely convinced of this fact, we will experience an outflow unlike anything we have yet experienced. Unfortunately, many still think that we are responsible for the fruit. It is true that God uses yielded hearts and lives as His instruments and as vehicles for His will, but to presume that we are the source is wrong. We can do nothing outside of God's unmerited favor upon our lives. The anointing flows in and through our lives as He gives the enablement.

Unless you find your place of habitation in the vine, you are a wayward branch and will be deemed useless. In fact, unless you're connected to the vine, you aren't a branch at all. You're nothing but an ugly stick. Without your life Source, you have no nourishment. Soon, all of your leaves will dry up and fall off. Your bark will lose its moisture and begin to crack and split. Nothing will be left, except a bitter, dried-up stick. No matter how much you strive to produce, without the Source of all life, no fruit will be found in you.

Within the principle of abiding there's no room for the "loner" mentality. No one person or ministry has the privilege to think they walk alone or hold the answer to the Kingdom or the world. It all goes back to the diamond. If the diamond were a flat rock, it wouldn't have any beauty. Its strength and its beauty rest in its many facets.

The Church, when working together, is a beautiful display of the many sides of Christ. The Body shows forth the brilliance of His character. When one part thinks it alone has all the answers, however, every part is in danger of being uprooted and cut off. Sooner or later, not only will it be convinced that it doesn't need the rest of the Body, but it will be beguiled and deceived, thinking itself to be important and cutting itself off from God.

Several years ago, when the Lord first began opening doors for me to travel and speak, I found I needed a biography letter. I'll never forget the words and counsel of Dr. Charlotte Baker. She told me, "Never believe your biography (what people say about you). The moment you do, you will begin to think you are somebody."

Jesus was not only teaching the disciples about abiding, He was also illustrating to them that when they abide, they produce. The ability of a fruit-bearing tree to produce fruit is not something it finds hard to accomplish. Apple trees don't strive to produce apples. It's their nature to produce apples. The same is true for us. When we are abiding in the vine, there's no reason to strive to produce. The problem is that we want to produce on our own timetable. Often our timetable and God's timetable are different. There is a time for all things under Heaven, and God knows that time.

Jesus is not only the vine in which we are to abide, but He is also the husbandman. Husbandry is "the art of cultivation, preparation and regeneration." It involves "a keen eye, a gentle, but strong touch and a good understanding of what is hidden beneath the soil." For a plant to survive, it must have a balance of sunlight, water, nourishment and pruning. The husbandman knows each and every plant. He is careful to watch over it for any signs of distress. He knows just when to repot, fertilize and prune. Most plants, if kept in healthy conditions, will flourish and grow.

Often, the kind of care a husbandman chooses to apply can seem catastrophic. Plants do not like to change. When change occurs, they often enter a stage of shock. Usually they recover, and thus the change becomes permanent.

Jesus used the word *"purge"* in relation to the care of the branches (see John 15:2). He said, *"Now ye are clean through the word which I have spoken to you"* (verse 3). With this, the reader understands that Jesus isn't speaking about the art of gardening, but about the principles of sanctification, preparation and admonition, to bring forth ripe fruit in due season.

Throughout the process of abiding, there are various stages of growth and change. Pruning, or purging, isn't easy. Indeed, it's ugly and uncomfortable. No one likes to be pruned. It leaves you stripped and bare, for everyone to see. You stick out like a weed in a beautiful garden. The process of pruning and exposure, however, is vital to every believer.

Pruning is easier to endure in private. We often embrace God's correction as long as no one is around to see or hear. But exposure means growth, and growth means maturity. Maturity means character, and character is never made in secret, because it takes other people, through trials, testings, strippings and dealings, to accomplish it.

I can't tell you how many times my foot has ended up in my mouth all the way to my waist — times when God has stepped back and openly allowed me to experience frustration, irritation and exasperation. I am grateful now, for His work has pruned me, and I'll never forget. Have my days of pruning finished? No. For as long as one walks and abides, there will be pruning.

If you wish to walk as a son or daughter, you cannot bypass any stage of admonition. The word *admonition* speaks of "discipline that relates to the training of a child." It also means "to call to attention." Only a constant balance of encouragement and reproof can bring about maturity.

If we are truly sons of God, the writer of Hebrews shows us, we can expect reproof:

> *If ye endure chastening, God dealeth with you as with sons; for what son is he whom the father chasteneth not? But if ye be without chastisement, whereof all are partakers, then are ye bastards, and not sons.*
>
> Hebrews 12:7-8

Abiding, the Key to Relationship

God is preparing us to produce. He wants us to walk in the full knowledge of His character and likeness.

Our fruit is not for making a show, but reflects the relationship we have in abiding. Every piece of fruit reveals a work of grace that has been developed in our lives. Fruit is to be eaten. You shouldn't try to grow fruit unless you're willing for it to be tasted. If you desire fruit simply for people to see how wonderful you are, then go buy wax fruit and hang it on your branches. But remember, when people taste it, they'll know if it's real or not and what source it came from.

If you connect yourself to bitterness, you'll produce a bitter fruit. If you harbor feelings of unforgiveness or jealousy, your fruit will be hard and dry.

The principle of abiding finds its place in the very heart of God. God has always wanted a people in whom He could abide. Whether it was in the garden, in the Tabernacle in the wilderness, in the simplicity of a tent, or in the hearts of men, God is an ever-abiding God. Our dependency must be in Him if we are going to carry the torch for our generation. Our dependency cannot be in anything or anyone else. It must be only in Jehovah God. Jeremiah warned:

> *Thus saith the* LORD; *Cursed be the man that trusteth in man, and maketh flesh his arm, and whose heart departeth from the* LORD. *For he shall be like the heath in the desert, and shall not see when good cometh; but shall inhabit the parched places in the wilderness, in a salt land and not inhabited. Blessed is the man that trusteth in the* LORD, *and whose hope the* LORD *is. For*

> *he shall be as a tree planted by the waters, and that spreadeth out her roots by the river, and shall not see when heat cometh, but her leaf shall be green; and shall not be careful in the year of drought, neither shall cease from yielding fruit.* Jeremiah 17:5-8

Jeremiah gives a clear description of those who rely on the flesh. They will be cursed. He gives a picture of desolation and spiritual drought. When you rely on the flesh, you lose your relationship with the Vine, and you cannot survive without relationship.

God warned Adam and Eve that breaking their covenant relationship with Him would bring death. To Adam, natural death must have seemed like a welcome relief. I cannot image how terrible it must have been to have walked with God in the relationship that he had enjoyed, only to experience complete separation when he fell. When we walk after the way of man, we create a gulf between God and ourselves.

The Scriptures state that we are blessed when we trust in the Lord. We will be *"as a tree planted by the waters."* Our roots will spread out by the river. We will not see when the heat comes; our leaf will not wither in drought, and we will not cease from yielding fruit. In this one passage we see that heat and drought will come, but when we are abiding in God, our roots will spread forth and we will produce.

Abiding in God puts us in a position of trust. In these last days, turmoil is all around us. Trust is the ingredient that carries us through the darkest hours.

Abiding, the Key to Relationship

When you abide in the Lord, you reflect His likeness. There's an old belief that married couples begin to look alike after many years of marriage. I don't know if it's true or not, in regards to the natural or physical, but concerning the principle of abiding, when a couple spends time together, face to face, they know each other's heart, mind, will and emotions. They even finish each other's sentences, because they know each other so well. This is the relationship we need to have with the Father, one that comes from many years of abiding in Him.

Twelve

According to Plumb

Thus he shewed me: and, behold, the Lord stood upon a wall made by a plumbline, with a plumbline in his hand. And the LORD said unto me, Amos, what seest thou? And I said, A plumbline. Then said the Lord, Behold, I will set a plumbline in the midst of my people Israel: I will not again pass by them any more. Amos 7:7-8

God is preparing us to carry the weight of His glory upon our shoulders as the priests of old carried the ark of His presence. For the past year I've been telling my congregation that every time I go to the Lord, He is requiring more of me. One more time He is putting His finger on areas I thought I had dealt with. He wants to see if I have completely died in that area, or if it has simply scabbed over. During this time, God led me to the book of Matthew. As I looked at the scripture concerning the Kingdom of God and His Kingdom principles, one portion seemed to be seared into my spirit:

> *Ye are the salt of the earth: but if the salt have lost his savour, wherewith shall it be salted? it is thenceforth good for nothing, but to be cast out, and to be trodden under foot of men.* Matthew 5:13

When I first approached the word *"savour,"* it was halfheartedly. I associated it with the sense of taste. Only recently did I begin to look at this scripture in light of God's dealings, and I saw the gravity of this word. Without savour, salt is *"good for nothing, but to be cast out, and to be trodden under foot of men."* These are strong words concerning God's expectations for us and how we are to walk on this Earth.

Savour finds its origin in God Himself. It is not simply a word we use to describe how something smells or tastes. In the Song of Solomon we read:

> *Because of the savour of thy good ointments thy name is as ointment poured forth, therefore do the virgins love thee.* Song of Solomon 1:3

God's name is associated directly with ointment and savour. Savour, completely defined, speaks of "the value, the substance, the usefulness and the effectiveness of the object that is tasted." Savour is "the measure or the quality of a substance that affects the sense of taste or smell. It has the power to excite, or repel, and it is distinctive." Savour, according to the Word of God, is a vital part of judgement. When God reestablished creation through Noah, He did so because of sacrifice and because of the savour:

> *And Noah builded an altar unto the LORD; and took of every clean beast, and of every clean fowl, and offered burnt offerings on the altar. And the LORD smelled A SWEET SAVOUR; and the LORD said in his heart, I will not again curse the ground any more for man's sake; for the imagination of man's heart is evil from his youth; neither will I again smite any more every thing living, as I have done. While the earth remaineth, seedtime and harvest, and cold and heat, and summer and winter, and day and night shall not cease.* Genesis 8:20-22

God used the *savour* to determine the quality of the sacrifice. Everything we do and all that we are produces a *savour.* In Romans 12:1 we're taught to present our bodies as a living sacrifice, holy and acceptable unto God. He is making an evaluation of our sacrifice, "savouring" the aroma that we offer up to Him daily. It can either be the sweet savour of relationship, acceptable to Him, or the stench of perspiration and the striving of our own endeavor.

We have not been called to walk around in this world aimlessly, but we are to change our surroundings. Just as salt changes whatever it touches, we are called to change the atmosphere about us simply by being God's salt in any given situation. Before we can ever be God's salt, however, we must allow Him to salt our lives with

His dealings. As His instruments, we have the ability to excite other individuals toward the things of God, or to repel them.

If we lose our *savour,* it means that we will have lost the ointment of His name. In that case, we will have lost the aroma of His presence in our lives, and we will be deemed useless. It is imperative for us to walk bearing the name of God. He wants to write His name upon us, but He cannot, and will not, if we don't possess the sweet aroma of sacrifice. Being the temple of God, we cannot have any agreement with idols (see 2 Corinthians 6:16-18).

Throughout the history of Israel, God was continually speaking to His children concerning His holy temple. From the beginning of time, He desired to dwell in man, but as a result of man's disobedience, God implemented a divine plan of redemption. In order for Him to dwell with man, He established a relationship through His temple. This did not begin at the Temple in Jerusalem, but in the Tabernacle in the wilderness.

When the children of Israel were delivered out of Egypt, God gave his servant Moses a plan. This elaborate plan involved the furnishings, the curtains, the sacrifices, a priesthood and a system of measure. Everything had to be done according to God's specific instructions. Nothing could be overlooked, neglected or passed over. Even the individual tribes had to be positioned correctly.

Over time, a simple tent replaced this Tabernacle in the wilderness, and King David eventually saw the need for God to have a permanent house. This conviction drove David to recover the ark from its wandering and place it in a tent, until such time as the permanent dwelling could be readied.

On the day that David decided to retrieve the ark, he set forth on a journey. He took the ark from the house of Abinadab in Gibeah and placed it upon a new cart. David and all those who accompanied him began to play their instruments and to shout and to rejoice. Then the oxen came to the threshing floor of Nachon and stumbled, and Uzza put forth his hand to steady the ark and keep it from falling. God's anger was kindled against him, and he was struck dead (see 2 Samuel 6 and 1 Chronicles 13).

The threshing floor was a place that was used to prepare the grain from the harvest. Oxen threshed the grain, treading it under their hooves, crushing the husks and releasing the kernels. These same oxen tripped on the threshing floor, even though it was a place they should have known. We may conclude from this that God was making a point. He wanted to teach David that He had an order and a plan, and that His order and plan had to be followed.

Every one of us recognizes the need for God's presence, but we don't always recognize that God has a divine order and a plan in all things. Having failed in his effort to bring the ark home, David went back and fell on his face, seeking God's order (see 1 Chronicles 15). Whenever we follow God's plan, keeping His standards, He blesses us with His presence.

God inspected the Tabernacle of Moses and afterward He chose to dwell there. On the day Solomon dedicated the Temple in Jerusalem, God entered in a mighty way, but only after He had inspected it thoroughly.

> *Then the house was filled with a cloud, even the house of the LORD; so that the priests could not stand to minister by reason of the cloud: for the glory of the LORD had filled the house of God.* 2 Chronicles 5:13-14

Whenever God's presence begins to be revealed in His temple, whether it's corporately or individually, many things begin to take place. First, He doesn't approach anything unless it has been dedicated and cleansed. We call this the washing in the blood of the Lamb. God provided for you and me the blood of His dear Son so that we could be washed and cleansed from all unrighteousness.

God's righteousness is given freely and is imputed to us by faith. The only responsibility we have is to remain in Him. There is an old phrase that says "We were saved, we are saved, and we will be saved." This statement reflects the continual work of grace in our lives, which brings us to the second point.

Whenever God's presence is revealed, He begins His work of judgement, or setting things in order. Today, the judgement of the Church is generally disregarded or ignored, since, as was mentioned in Chapter Seven, it's considered an Old Testament work. Because we live under God's covenant of grace and mercy, we seldom recognize our need for true judgement. Judgement for the Church is based on who God is, rather than on a system of works or on the Law. This judgement is based on the holiness of God, and this holiness calls for separation.

According to Plumb

In his book of Revelation, John received a series of messages from Jesus for seven churches. In each message, God pronounced judgement, based on His holiness. In Pergamos, Thyatira and Sardis, His judgement separated the holy from the profane. In Ephesus, Philadelphia and Laodicea, God judged holiness in relationship. To the faithful of Smyrna, He awarded life.

As the temple of God, we cannot escape or slip past the judgement of God. No temple in history ever has. When God's presence is revealed, He ushers forth a work of sanctification. Sanctification is a word that is seldom used today, because it points to old fashioned repentance. Sanctification, however, involves cleansing, and no one can escape God's cleansing. A true work of sanctification is an operation of the Holy Spirit by which He applies the water of the Word as we surrender to Him. Thus, we are cleansed and set apart for divine use.

On one occasion, God used a plumb line for judgement. A plumb line is used to determine the perpendicularity (establishing a vertical upright) of an object. It is used to measure the depth of water, or it can also be used to make a straight vertical line, which is important for construction.

God showed the prophet Amos a plumb line in His hand:

> *Thus he shewed me: and, behold, the Lord stood upon a wall made by a plumbline, with a plumbline in his hand. And the* Lord *said unto me, Amos, what seest thou? And I said, A plumbline. Then said the Lord,*

People of His Presence

Behold, I will set a plumbline in the midst of my people Israel: I will not again pass by them any more.
Amos 7:7-8

The standard God uses is upright. By showing Amos that the wall was plumb, He established not only that we are to conform to a standard, but that we are to be a standard for others. In God, there is no room for mixture, nor is there any room for bending or bowing. We are to be an upright standard in the midst of a wicked and perverse generation. God never compares us to something that is based on any bias or slant. He always uses an upright standard. Once we are established, we will become a standard for others.

Arise, shine; for thy light is come, and the glory of the L*ORD is risen upon thee. For, behold, the darkness shall cover the earth, and gross darkness the people: but the* L*ORD shall arise upon thee, and his glory shall be seen upon thee.* Isaiah 60:1-2

God's glory cannot and will not show forth from anything unholy. The glory of God will be seen upon us as a garment as we allow Him to enlarge Himself in us. We will become a standard, a light for all to see and salt for all to savour.

We are God's dwelling place, and as His dwelling place, we cannot escape His standard. Whenever God is revealed, if we are straddling the fence, it will be easily seen. When He reveals His presence, we have to make a choice. We can either walk as a *People of His Presence* or walk as a religious people.

Taking on a religious identification is worse than walking in complete darkness. If we walk in the mere acknowledgment of truth, but refuse to allow truth to work in us and through us, we will be guilty of the sin of Laodicea, the lukewarm church of Revelation, that seemed unable to distinguish between hot and cold. Or, like Laodicea, we may be found boasting that we are rich in material wealth while ignoring our spiritual poverty. When God's presence is revealed, He comes as the refiner's fire to try us as gold, so that we may walk richly in His Kingdom.

Looking at the life of Jesus, I understand why He didn't seem to mind being around sinners. At least they are honest in their approach to sin and to God. They don't hide or pretend that they are something they aren't.

However, their world has no set of principles or moral standards by which to be governed. To sinners anything goes, anything is allowed, because in the kingdom of darkness, Satan is their father. The world is not doing anything wrong according to the system that governs it. One of the biggest errors the Church makes is to look at the world and judge it according to God's standards. His standards do not apply to sinners unless they choose to live under His roof.

I grew up hearing my father say, "As long as you live under my roof, you'll do as I say." The same goes for the Kingdom of God. If we live under God's roof, the activities of the world and the opinions of the world don't apply to us.

Religious hypocrisy brings a reproach to the Kingdom of God. Sinners see the Church living by two sets of standards. They see us dabble in the kingdom of darkness, and then go to a church on Sunday. This hypocrisy makes a stench. God isn't just for an hour on Sunday. He isn't an object for pomp and circumstance. Religion is not intended to set us on a pedestal so that we can then look down on the rest of the world because of its sin. Jesus addressed this in the situation of the woman who was caught in adultery. He looked at the crowd and indicated that anyone who did not have sin could cast the first stone. How often do we, as Christians, sit as judge and jury over the heathen and ignore the sin in our own lives?

I would take a good sinner any day, rather than a religious hypocrite. Godly conviction should begin in the house of the Lord and then flow out to the dying world. The world will see true conviction on the day that we walk as a convicted people.

When the waters of God start to rise, He will drop a plumb line to measure the depth. Several years ago, God gave me a vision of His coming glory. He took me by the Spirit to the edge of a great body of water. As I stood looking upon the water, I began to see the faces of many people standing at the water's edge. I listened to the crowd as they cried, "Send Your presence."

As people made their cry known, I noticed that a small number of them looked up, while the multitude looked to the horizon. At first glance, I thought the individuals who were looking out at the horizon, as the waves rolled around their ankles, would be the first ones to see God's presence coming in the distance. As they watched the horizon, the water began to rise and ripple in a gentle breeze that was now blowing. I began to hear them exclaim with great excitement, "It's here. What our hearts have longed for has come."

The water that had been filled with waves appeared to be very high, but upon closer examination, it was only an illusion of movement that made it appear deep. The people continued to shout with great joy and excitement as the water wet their garments and splashed upon their hair.

Then the Lord turned my eyes to a small group of individuals who had been standing in the water with their eyes focused upward. The water rippled and splashed, and the wind blew all around them, but their eyes didn't break from their upward stare. They were fixed, like statues, and didn't change their posture. Soon the water they were standing in began to rise. It was ankle deep, then knee deep, waist deep and shoulder deep, until it covered them entirely. Never once did they change their focus.

As I looked at the water, it looked like a translucent sea of glass, and the individuals who were covered were still visible to the natural eye. Just then I began to see wheelchairs, crutches and chains floating in the water all around them. Instantly, I realized that the individuals who had watched the horizon, as the sun slowly fell, were only interested in the end result, what the water had produced.

The rising water, however, was for those who surrendered to it. The water wasn't just to splash around in, but for swimming. Water is for life. It's to purify, wash, restore, heal and refresh. If we desire the benefits of God, then we need to be ready to experience everything the water has to offer.

As the waters of God's presence begin to rise, God will drop a plumb line to measure our depths. Many times we appear to be in deep water until a crisis comes. Then, suddenly, it's as if the plug has been pulled. God often uses life's circumstances to test how deep we are in His truths. The truth we have must be tested in the circumstances of life.

Several years ago we were faced with some financial struggles. I wish I could say I passed every test with flying colors, but that isn't the case. I knew that God was a God of provision, but He tested me to see if I really believed what I professed. One day during this trial, my husband came home with a bit of news that I didn't want to hear. It was the straw that broke the camel's back, as they say. I started to cry, and then I started to rant and rave in a way that only a woman knows how. My husband proceeded to rehearse, in my ears, all the things that he had heard me preach, time and time again. I had just finished a series called "God Is a God of Provision." Hearing him, I really got upset! It was like gasoline had been poured on an open flame, and there wasn't any water to extinguish the fire.

I knew I had to get hold of myself, and I had to get hold of God too. I spent the next several days on my face before God and I went through one of those gut-wrenching moments when you come face-to-face with the truth. By the end of my search, I found God in the midst of my struggle. When I arose, I knew I had met with the One who is above all circumstance. He had put His ax to the root and cut out all of those areas that I thought I had under control (or should I say, "under my control"). I learned firsthand that God wanted to be in control. He had used a circumstance to test the depth of my waters and to see if I would trust Him through my struggle, or if my struggle would cause me to falter in the Word of God, even though I knew it was true.

About two weeks later my husband came home again with a bit of news. I remember it as if it were yesterday. I was standing at the stove cooking dinner when he asked, "So, do you want the good news or the bad news?"

I turned to him and said, "You know it really doesn't matter."

He looked at me rather strangely, as if to say, "I'm sure expecting another scene." As he stood there, telling me the news, I looked at him and began to sing, "He'll Do It Again." I sang out loudly, "Just like Moses, just like Daniel, just like Shadrach, Meshach, and Abednego, He'll do it again."

My husband stood there, shocked, and asked me, "What happened to you?"

I told him I had met the God of all circumstances, and God is God, no matter what comes our way.

Several weeks later my husband came home and asked, "So … do you want the good news?" and he told me, "God came through!"

Through this trial I came to understand firsthand that the depths of our waters aren't based on testimony, and they aren't based on experience, but that the water of God's presence comes upon us through relationship. The depth of our spiritual experience is established on the living reality that God is God, no matter what comes or what goes.

God is on the move. He is cutting through formalities. He is penetrating our traditions and drawing people closer to Himself. He is measuring the depths of our waters, smelling the savour from our lives. We can choose to hold on to man's ways and ideas of religious truth and be deemed lukewarm and good for nothing, or we can become the salt of this Earth, with the sweet savour of the Eternal One.

Part Four

The Treasure

THIRTEEN

AS OINTMENT POURED FORTH

Because of the savour of thy good ointments thy name is as ointment poured forth, therefore do the virgins love thee. Song of Solomon 1:3

One of the ways that God uses to reveal Himself to man is through His name. This is a timeless subject that reaches through eternity. Despite the numerous books that have been written on the subject, we have only scratched the surface of the depths of God's nature. He is the Eternal One, the Everlasting and the Ancient of Days.

God, who is the initiator of relationship, gives us His Word to help us grasp His infinite name. His name will stand forever. His name is like His nature. It is multifaceted. He has many names! At the dawning of the coming age, He will, in fact, reveal a new name that no man knows, only He, Himself.

> *His eyes were as a flame of fire, and on his head were many crowns; and he had a name written, that no man knew, but he himself.* Revelation 19:12

This means that there will never be an end to discovering and seeing God in fresh and exciting ways. Just think, we'll have all eternity to learn to know His name and all of its many facets. God's name gives us a glimpse into His very character and His very nature. The Scriptures describe:

> *The heavens declare the glory of God; and the firmament sheweth his handywork. Day unto day uttereth speech, and night unto night sheweth knowledge. There is no speech nor language, where their voice is not heard. Their line is gone out through all the earth, and their words to the end of the world. In them hath he set a tabernacle for the sun, which is as a bridegroom coming out of his chamber, and rejoiceth as a strong man to run a race. His going forth is from the end of the heaven, and his circuit unto the ends of it: and there is nothing hid from the heat thereof.*
>
> Psalm 19:1-6

God's name is established throughout the ends of the Earth. Everything He does, speaks to us about who He is. I am convinced that God is moving in our midst to reveal and establish us concerning who He is. When darkness fills the Earth and gross darkness the people, many will be running about seeking peace. If we are going to be a *People of His Presence,* we must know who it is in whom we have believed. We need to be able to point others to Him, without having any doubt in ourselves.

> *That Christ may dwell in your hearts by faith; that ye, being rooted and grounded in love, may be able to comprehend with all saints what is the breadth, and length, and depth, and height; and to know the love of Christ, which passeth knowledge, that ye might be filled with all the fulness of God.*
>
> Ephesians 3:17-19

You and I have the ability to know the breadth, length, depth and height of God. He doesn't withhold any part of Himself from us. There is only one requirement: that we be rooted and grounded in love.

When God's name is poured forth, it's a sweet ointment. It has within it everything that we need. He tells us, in His name, ask; in His name, believe; in His name, cast out; in His name, trust. Everything we could possibly need is locked within His name.

All provision rests within Jehovah-Jireh, God who provides. In Genesis 22, He established Himself as the God who will always provide when He provided the ram for sacrifice in place of Isaac. God's provision goes beyond our need. It's like a parent's love for a child. The child might need something, but the parent's desire to provide it will always surpass the child's desire. That is why God provides what we need, not necessarily what we ask for. There is a great difference between need and desire, as any parent knows.

When Jesus came to Earth, He became further proof of the providential nature of God. On the cross, He became the ultimate provision for us, sealing God's redemption for mankind, once and for all. He tells us that we have overcome the adversary *"by the blood of the Lamb, and by the word of [our] testimony"* (Revelation 12:11). This means that we can overcome by the very nature of God. He is our provider, and He has provided for Satan's defeat.

The name of the Lord is always related to the Word of God and to the Spirit of God:

> *For there are three that bear record in heaven, the Father, the Word, and the Holy Ghost: and these three are one.* 1 John 5:7

Years ago, a man's word was sealed with his name. When a man vowed a vow he backed this vow with everything that was in him. When God sent Moses, He instructed him to tell the people: *"I AM hath sent me unto you"* (Exodus 3:14). When God sends you to do something, you can rest assured that it's always bigger than you are and greater than you can accomplish on your own. But we have this confidence, that the I AM is always with us. God cannot be anything but faithful. It would be against everything that He is to be anything less.

> *And righteousness shall be the girdle of his loins, and FAITHFULNESS the girdle of his reins.* Isaiah 11:5

As Ointment Poured Forth

Know therefore that the Lord *thy God, he is God, the FAITHFUL God.* Deuteronomy 7:9

Thy mercy, O Lord*, is in the heavens; and thy FAITHFULNESS reacheth unto the clouds.* Psalm 36:5

God is not a man, that he should lie; neither the son of man, that he should repent: hath he said, and shall he not do it? or hath he spoken, and shall he not make it good? Numbers 23:19

God reveals Himself so that we can become like Him. He is always unveiling, revealing and enlarging Himself in us. When He makes His presence known to us, He is, in essence, pouring out His name. His presence, when manifested, will always contain and show forth His name and who He is. His presence will always contain an element of creation (Elohim), cleansing (M'Kaddesh), healing (Rophe) and righteousness (Tsidkenu), to name a few. Anything apart from God's name isn't God. His presence is being poured out upon the Earth, but not everything that claims to be God is God.The time has come for the Church to be wise concerning the name of God. It's time to know Him in His fullness.

FOURTEEN

ESTEEMING THE TREASURE WITHIN

But we have this treasure in earthen vessels.
2 Corinthians 4:7

Despite Adam's disobedience, God chose man to carry His glory. When you receive Jesus into your heart, you become a messenger [container] of His beautiful treasure:

> *Who being the brightness of his glory, and the express image of his person, and upholding all things by the word of his power, when he had by himself purged our sins, sat down on the right hand of the Majesty on high; being made so much better than the angels, as he hath by inheritance obtained a more excellent name than they.* Hebrews 1:3-4

Jesus is the only liaison between God and man. The covenants of God were instruments that God used to bring man into a place of relationship with Himself. In every covenant, He sought to restore man to his rightful place. The covenants, however, worked on people from the outside in. But when Jesus came, He took the covenant system that had worked from the outside and placed it within man. Jesus became the mediator of the covenant. Today, for you and me, God's covenants are not only a type or a shadow, but they are fulfilled in the life of Jesus:

> *And for this cause he is the mediator of the new testament, that by means of death, for the redemption of the transgressions that were under the first testament, they which are called might receive the promise of eternal inheritance.* Hebrews 9:15

Another portion from Hebrews shows a dynamic aspect of Jesus' ministry:

> *His Son, whom he hath appointed heir of all things.*
> Hebrews 1:2

Jesus then, by inheritance, is the *"heir of all things."* If you can grasp the meaning of this statement, you will realize that everything that Jesus has, is yours: *"And if children, then heirs; heirs of God, and joint-heirs with Christ"* (Romans 8:17).

Our treasure rests in who Jesus is. It isn't an empty chest of dreams, nor is it a treasure that will someday loose its value. Jesus is the keeper of all God's promises. God has sealed His words with the blood of His very own Son. This is an idea that is often hard to receive or believe. More than a few times in life people have made promises to us and then broken them. The language of the human race is full of apologies, excuses and downright fabrications (which is a big word that sounds better than saying we're liars). Because of this, we have trouble believing that God can and does keep every one of His promises. He doesn't play with our emotions, nor does He dangle us over a barrel. He completes everything that He has promised.

There is, however, one variable that enters this formula that we cannot forget to mention, and that variable is *me*, and in your case, *you*. God's promises carry with them all the power necessary to accomplish their task. There are times, though, when the promise may be withheld because of the decisions people make in their lives. This doesn't mean that God places an "out" clause within His promises so that He can get off the hook. It simply means that some of the responsibility for the completion of His promises in our lives belongs to us and that disobedience can ruin His plan for us.

Because God is not a man, we can place our entire trust in Him. What more assurance do we need than the Word of God, the name of God, and the character of God? *"We have this treasure in earthen vessels"* (2 Corinthians 4:7). There is a treasure within us. This is our hope and our confidence. In Him, we can rest secure:

> *Come unto me, all ye that labour and are heavy laden, and I will give you rest. Take my yoke upon you, and*

learn of me; for I am meek and lowly in heart: and ye shall find rest unto your souls. For my yoke is easy, and my burden is light. Matthew 11:28-30

When we walk in the knowledge of Christ, we will show forth the radiance of God:

Arise, shine; for thy light is come, and the glory of the LORD *is risen upon thee.* Isaiah 60:1

When we embrace Jesus, who is the light, we express the beauty of God. This is not an uncertainty; it's a solemn fact.

The necessity of understanding that none of our humanity will ever attain divine status is vital. We will not become "little gods." He has commissioned us to express His image from the inside out. We are God's instruments, but never did He intend for us to be raised to the place of being worshiped. There is a fine line between admiration and worship.

It is okay to admire someone, but when admiration causes us to look to a man for approval, rather than to God, we're in danger of sinning. Only God should be worshiped.

I personally believe that Christian award shows may cross this line between admiration and worship. It seems that the Church may be falling into idolatry, just like the world. Have we gotten to the place that we look to man to meet our needs rather than to God? Do we look to man, and worship man's words, and place man above God? God forbid!

Jesus cleansed the Temple in Jerusalem:

> *And they come to Jerusalem: and Jesus went into the temple, and began to cast out them that sold and bought in the temple, and overthrew the tables of the moneychangers, and the seats of them that sold doves; and would not suffer that any man should carry any vessel through the temple.* Mark 11:15-16

On the day Jesus entered the Temple, His heart ached because of what He saw. He became angry at the abominations that were taking place inside the Temple. Many times, when we have read the account of Jesus cleansing the Temple, we've only noticed the fact that He removed the moneychangers. However, He was cleansing far more:

> *Thus saith the LORD, Keep ye judgment, and do justice: for my salvation is near to come, and my righteousness to be revealed. Blessed is the man that doeth this, and the son of man that layeth hold on it; THAT KEEPETH THE SABBATH FROM POLLUTING IT, AND KEEPETH HIS HAND FROM DOING ANY EVIL. NEITHER LET THE SON OF THE STRANGER, THAT HATH JOINED HIMSELF TO THE LORD, SPEAK, SAYING, THE LORD HATH UTTERLY SEPARATED ME FROM HIS PEOPLE: neither let the eunuch say, Behold, I am a dry tree. For thus saith the LORD unto the eunuchs that keep my sabbaths, and choose the things that please me, and take hold of my covenant; even*

> *unto them will I* GIVE IN MINE HOUSE AND WITHIN MY WALLS A PLACE AND A NAME BETTER THAN OF SONS AND OF DAUGHTERS: I WILL GIVE THEM AN EVERLASTING NAME, THAT SHALL NOT BE CUT OFF. *Also the sons of the stranger, that join themselves to the* LORD*, to serve him, and to love the name of the* LORD*, to be his servants, every one that keepeth the sabbath from polluting it, and taketh hold of my covenant; even them will I bring to my holy mountain, and make them joyful in my house of prayer:* THEIR BURNT OFFERINGS AND THEIR SACRIFICES SHALL BE ACCEPTED UPON MINE ALTAR; FOR MINE HOUSE SHALL BE CALLED AN HOUSE OF PRAYER FOR ALL PEOPLE. Isaiah 56:1-7

There were several things Jesus saw when He entered the Temple. First, it was a house divided against itself. It wasn't a house for all people or nations. There was a separate court for the Gentiles, the priests, the women, the men, the Nazarites and the lepers.

Second, instead of offering sacrifices, the people were buying and selling. They didn't deem the house sacred, nor did they keep the Sabbath free from pollution.

The third abomination was that the Israelites were bringing foreign vessels into the house.

> *So they came to Jerusalem. Then Jesus went into the temple and began to drive out those who bought and sold in the temple, and overturned the tables of the money changers and the seats of those who sold doves.*

Esteeming the Treasure Within

> *And He would not allow anyone to carry wares through the temple.* Mark 11:15-16, NKJ

Jesus was fulfilling all that was written in Isaiah when He cleansed the Temple:

> *And he taught, saying unto them, Is it not written, My house shall be called of all nations the house of prayer? but ye have made it a den of thieves.*
> Mark 11:17

When the Father looks at His temple today, I hope He doesn't see the same abominations. We must be careful to guard and esteem the treasure we have within us as precious. Jesus is the treasure! As we walk bearing His name, let us take care not to bring shame to Him.

FIFTEEN

CHANGED FROM GLORY TO GLORY

We all ... are changed into the same image from glory to glory. 2 Corinthians 3:18

Several years ago, I heard the Spirit of the Lord say to me, "What you behold, you will become." At that moment I felt Him touch my eyes, and immediately I felt His hand beginning to purge my life to an even greater degree. I am convinced that whatever my eyes see, I will become. This is a twofold work. It takes place in the natural, as well as in the spiritual.

God is in the process of establishing Himself within the midst of His Church. With this, God brings an awareness of His throne. A throne is an interesting place. It represents authority. God's throne also represents justice, mercy and judgement. It is a place from which all things in a kingdom are ruled and governed. When we give a place to something or entertain it, we give it a right to set up its seat of authority (throne) within us.

When Korah entertained the thought that he could do things just as well as Moses, he established a seat of rebellion, which became a throne in his life and led to his utter destruction (see Numbers 16). When God spoke to me that what I beheld I would become, I knew it involved the principle of changing in Him:

> *But we all, with open face beholding as in a glass the glory of the* Lord, *are changed into the same image from glory to glory, even as by the Spirit of the Lord.*
> 2 Corinthians 3:18

Looking at this scripture, several things are apparent. First, we *"ALL"* must behold. No one can escape the process of change. Adam's sin has ravished creation, and every creature must be transformed, that is, changed, into the image of God.

Secondly, something is given for us to look into, like a *"glass"* (mirror). God's mirror isn't like ours. It shows a picture, not of what we are, but of what we are to become as we continue to look at Him. The Word of God is often referred to as a mirror, because it shows us who we are to become. When I choose, out of obedience, to look into the mirror of God's Word, He shows Himself to me. He doesn't reflect my sin, my failures or my struggles, but He points me to Himself. God never looks at us without looking through His Son's blood. He always sees us through the imputed righteousness of Jesus.

The third point is that the process of change is through the working of the Spirit of God. We cannot accomplish this process of change by ourselves. When we get involved, we usually end up beating ourselves up, rather than changing.

Several years ago, I was personally struggling with the principle of change and of dying to self. I knew that God had His hand on me, and I was trying to die to anything and everything that was adversely affecting my spiritual life. Seeing my struggle, Dr. Baker told me, "Cindy, nail your left foot. Nail your right foot. Nail your left hand. Now, what are you going to do with your right hand? It's still out there, waving around." She explained that it was impossible to kill myself spiritually. It was the job of the Holy Spirit to do it. This was something I knew, but when it came down to allowing it to be done, I had thought I could help the Holy Spirit. In reality, the only thing I had to do was be willing and surrender.

"To withdraw" and "to die" are not synonymous. Just because you withdraw doesn't mean that you have died or changed. Change involves the process of death. It's not something you can bring about by yourself. Your part is to look into the mirror and to be completely surrendered to the process of change. Death involves the absence of life. When you truly die to something, no breath and no life are left.

God doesn't bring us to the place of change only to make a causal adjustment. Our culture revolves around change. We change hairstyles, clothing, cars and music, according to the style that society is dictating at any given time. These changes affect only the appearance and a person's projected image. They're supposedly used to relay to others how we feel, or how we want to feel.

Image is a big thing in our culture. How someone or something looks dictates whether or not a person is accepted. When it comes to the Kingdom of God, image takes on a completely different meaning.

On the day that Jesus was born, He took on an earthly form to walk this Earth. He is described for us in Isaiah as one with *"no form nor comeliness; and when we shall see him, there is no beauty that we should desire him"* (Isaiah 53:2). While on Earth, Jesus told His disciples and His followers, *"He that hath seen me hath seen the Father"* (John 14:9). Was Jesus speaking of what the disciples were seeing in the natural? Certainly not, because Jesus was the Son of man in the flesh.

When Jesus walked this Earth, He openly revealed who God was. With every word and deed, He revealed who it was that they were to become. Jesus knew that being a follower and a disciple meant change. He knew that it meant laying down everything, surrendering all, and leaving behind the most cherished *things.* When you become a follower of Jesus, you choose the eternal ways of God over your own ways. When Jesus was born, He knew what He was born to do: to die (see Isaiah 53). When He walked this Earth, He knew the Kingdom, and He knew the message He was to reveal: the message of the Kingdom (see Matthew 5-7 and John 12:49). When He healed, delivered and forgave, He knew that He was revealing His Father.

As followers of Christ, do we have our own agendas? Do we make Jesus follow our pattern? The throne of God was well established in Jesus. He did not strive against His Father's seat of authority that was within Him. He simply obeyed. When the world looks at the Church, can they tell that we're a reflection of God?

When you truly behold the cross, you will bear the marks of death. When you behold His blood, you will bear the marks of His redemption. When you spend time with Him, you will become like Him. When you spend time looking into His Word (mirror), you will become fashioned into the image that His Word shows. We are to walk as the revealed image of God. The image of the Word is Jesus. Jesus is the reflection of God. Every word He spoke was the Word of God.

For several months now the Spirit has kept me studying the life of Jesus. When we look at His life, valuable truths unfold that show us how we are to walk, what we are to do, how we are to live, and how we are to die.

When I look at Jesus, the Anointed One, I never see Him attempting to bring any fame or fortune to Himself. The life of Christ demonstrates how we are to conduct ourselves in every aspect of life.

When we are changed, we are changed into the very likeness and image of Jesus, who was the Son of man and the Son of God. When you experience the salvation of God, you are more than a son of man, you become a son of God. You receive the adoption of sonship by which you call Him Abba, Father. This transfers you from the kingdom of darkness into the Kingdom of God's dear Son. From that point forward, the process of change requires that the nature of the natural man or woman be surrendered to the nature of God. Before we do that, everything in us is walking contrary to the nature of God. But through obedience and the Holy Spirit, our lives can line up with God's image.

Sixteen

He Is Always Present

O God, when thou wentest forth before thy people, when thou didst march through the wilderness; Selah: the earth shook, the heavens also dropped at the presence of God: even Sinai itself was moved at the presence of God, the God of Israel. Psalm 68:7-8

From the beginning of time, God's presence has been the source of life from which all of His plans spring. In Genesis, His presence is seen in creation, as He moved across the face of the waters and as He breathed His breath into man. His presence was the source of relationship, as He talked with man in the garden, and later, as He spoke concerning the disobedience of man. His presence was also the source of redemption, when He took it upon Himself to clothe Adam and Eve's shame.

God's presence is not something that we speak of in terms of a force that happens to be out there somewhere.

His presence is a tangible life source for you and me. If we are to be a people who walk bearing the presence of God, it is necessary that we understand His presence. Whenever one refers to the presence of God, there are generally two perceptions — His omnipresence and His manifest presence — with the latter of the two being the greater concerning our personal experience.

The omnipresence of God, the characteristic of God that reveals His ever-abiding, always-present position in our midst, is a dynamic and powerful part of His nature. It is the part of God that is the very foundation from which all else is revealed. It is the omnipresence of God that we depend on to be constant. It is that attribute of God that tells us, "I will never leave thee, nor forsake thee." It is the promise that we have: *"Christ in you, the hope of glory."* His omnipresence is a fact that we can rely on and trust.

Whenever God chooses to reveal Himself in a tangible way, it's not that He has suddenly arrived, fallen or come in, rather it's that He, who is ever-present, has chosen to pull back the veil of flesh that hides Him from our view and has allowed us to see His ever-present position in our midst. When God allows His presence to be revealed into the dimension of man's senses, we call it the "manifest presence" of God.

When we think in terms of "suddenly," concerning the presence of God, it means not only that He comes quickly, but also that when He comes to us, He presents something new. Actually there is nothing "new" in God. He has always been! This is our source of safety. There is no new thing in God, just a fresh or new understanding for us, or a fresh dimension for us to know.

There's nothing new in God's character, as in something new being "created." When God reveals Himself in our midst, He is depositing a portion of Himself into the core of His people. It is at that point that the presence of God becomes tangible to us. We are then able to feel, see, smell and sense His presence.

As wonderful as His manifest presence is, there has been much controversy about what it really means. We have heard such phrases as "the wind of God," "the fire of God," "the river of God," and "the anointing of God." But have you ever seen anyone leave a service with singed hair, soaking wet or dripping in oil? These phrases have been used commonly to depict the movement of God within our places of worship, but exactly what do they mean? What are we trying to say by them? When we say that we're experiencing the "fire of God" or "a revival of fire," what are we trying to communicate? Do we use these phrases as mere adjectives to describe what we feel? Or do these phrases describe a part of who God is, not just what He does. When you say "the fire of God," are you speaking of a specific outpouring or movement of God?

Several types of fire are spoken of in the Word of God, and each one of them is specific. In Exodus, there was the burning bush where Moses received his commission (see Exodus 3). Then there was the pillar of fire, which guided the children of Israel in the wilderness (see Exodus 13). There was also the fire of worship and sacrifice, which lit the wood on the altar (see Leviticus 9:23-24). Fire came as an answer from God (see 1 Kings 18:24).

God is the refiner's fire, which came and purified the sons of Levi (see Malachi 3:2-3). In Revelation, He is the fire-eyed God (see Revelation 1:14).

God's outpourings are not just symbolic. These phrases communicate an experience and speak of attributes of God. A symbol is a figure, a representation, something that can be interpreted to represent something else. This means that in these examples the fire of God is more than a mere representation of God; it is God. The same is true of water, oil and wind.

Whenever we use these terms, we should know and understand that we are talking about more than an experience. We are speaking of God's very presence in our lives. When we say that He comes with fire, what we're really saying is that God, who is fire, has come and touched our lives with His very being.

God's fire has many properties. There are times when He comes as fire to answer us (see 1 Kings 18:24), to refine us (see Malachi 3), to consume our enemies (see Psalm 97), to baptize us (see Matthew 3:11 and Luke 3:16), to lead us (see Exodus 13), and to consume our sacrifice (see Leviticus 9:24), just to name a few.

The same is true in reference to the anointing, or the oil of God's presence. There are many properties to His anointing, each one reflecting a distinct part of His nature. His nature is to be applied to our very lives. Just as the oil is holy (see Exodus 30:25 and 31-32), we also are to be holy. The oil was beaten (see Exodus 29:40), and we, too, should experience the deep dealings of God in our lives. Beating released another characteristic of the oil. It was also perfumed (see Exodus 30:23-25). The oil was handcrafted (see Exodus 30:25).

He Is Always Present

When God makes a deposit of His anointing into our lives, He comes in and crafts us by His hand for His purposes. The presence of the anointing in a service isn't there only to be used as a tool for discerning what the speaker is teaching, nor is it there only to bless us. He comes with purpose! When we understand that the anointing is a Person, we will have the awareness that it is precious (see Proverbs 21:20), costly (see Mark 14:3), and of the finest quality (see Amos 6:6, Exodus 30:23 and Numbers 18:12).

God does not reveal Himself to give us a great experience or to give us a great testimony. He reveals Himself to change us, lead us, equip us, purge and cleanse us, wash us, set us apart and ignite us. Our flesh wants to see manifestations. We do not like to admit this fact, but unfortunately, it's true. It is very exciting to see, feel and experience God. But when we refuse to see past what He is doing, we will not receive what He is imparting.

When God reveals Himself to us, He is infusing us with Himself. We have the opportunity to become everything He is (that doesn't mean we become God Himself). We have the ability to become water, as we release the rivers of God that are within us to a dry and thirsty world. Within us is the well that will never run dry. If you know who He is who lives in you, then you can offer those around you a part of who you are. When you are the fire of God, you will show forth the fire and the zeal to those who are around you.

Your very life can be a witness of the pillar of fire that leads God's children through the darkness. Your life can be the wind, which blows life into the dry bones, causing wickedness to be uprooted and saving your generation.

The presence of God is real. It's not just another experience. It is life. Over the past several years there has been an increase in sights, sounds and experiences in God. Because of this, there has also been an increased hunger to see signs. From the beginning of Christ's ministry on Earth, signs and wonders followed Him and became a source of much fascination. On several occasions, Jesus told those who were around Him, who witnessed these manifestations, not to tell anybody what they had seen or heard (see Matthew 8:1-4, Matthew 17:9 and Mark 7:36).

Jesus knew the tendency of man to seek after signs, and He taught that in the last days people would run about looking to see Christ (see Matthew 24:23-24). In the Greek, Christ is the word *Christos,* and it means "anointing" or "anointed One." Could it be that the Lord was pointing to the problem we see today of people running from place to place looking for the anointing? If people continue to seek the manifestations of God, rather than seeking to know Him, they will be deceived, just as the Lord said they would be.

When things are loud and exciting, we think the anointing is great. If things are quiet, we tend to discount the presence of God. I'm afraid that the Church has become "sign-conscious" rather than "presence-conscious," and these two concepts are worlds apart.

Hours of soulish preaching, praise and prayer cannot replace one second in the true presence of God, when He reveals Himself in the midst of His Church. We are not to be a people led by our emotions, by the sights we see, or by the sounds we hear. They are often misleading and unreliable. God doesn't need to get His people pumped up for them to receive from Him. He doesn't need theatrical lights, singers or accompaniment — just a yielded heart.

The presence of God cannot be manipulated. It isn't a slogan to attract crowds, nor is it a gimmick to sell a product. The presence of God is God. It's not a reflection of Him; it is Him.

Whenever God reveals Himself through a sign, He does so to establish Himself within His people. When He turned the bitter waters to sweet, He told the Israelites to mark it as a statute and an ordinance, and He established Himself as their provider (see Exodus 15:25). Signs are for a specific purpose. They establish the very nature of God within us. God's presence is not for our personal entertainment; it's to change us and create in us the living reality that He is the very breath we breathe. He is our sustaining joy, when everything is falling in all around us. He is our peace in the midst of the raging sea. He is the fourth man in the fire, when the fire would consume us. He is the very life force, without which we cannot live.

God is always present. It is this deep well of relationship that carries us beyond life's greatest tests and struggles and allows us to show forth His unmerited favor and grace.

Sevent

The Testimony of Jesus

And I fell at his feet to worship him. And he said unto me, See thou do it not: I am thy fellowservant, and of thy brethren that have the testimony of Jesus: worship God: for the testimony of Jesus is the spirit of prophecy. Revelation 19:10

In understanding the presence of God, one cannot ignore the anointing or the element of prophecy, both of which are misunderstood and often separated from who God is. No structure is sound without a proper foundation.

Prophecy may be compared to a giant skyscraper in a big city. To some, it's a place of beauty and is necessary to the city's industry and life. To others, it is nothing more than an eyesore or a monstrosity, which everyone tries to ignore and apologize for, if it is even noticed.

/ is sometimes viewed as a gift to be apolo-
ıf it comes forth. When you take a close look at
cy, however, it isn't merely a gift or function, but
of God Himself.

One of the biggest reasons prophecy has been a great ource of contention within the Body of Christ is that its emphasis is seldom on God, but on man. Prophecy comes from the mouth of God: "God said..." He speaks His heart, mind, will and ways to man. When He speaks, His breath is released. This breath has within it the creative ability to accomplish the words that have been spoken.

When we look at prophecy, we often get caught up in the human element rather than focusing on the divine element. When true prophecy goes forth, God releases His person into the realm of man's comprehension, through sight and sound. God's person will be clearly manifest in all genuine prophecy, which will always reveal a portion of His nature and character. It may reveal elements of creation (Elohim), cleansing (Jehovah-M'Kaddesh), healing (Jehovah-Rophe), righteousness (Jehovah-Tsidkenu), provision (Jehovah-Jireh), or the God who is always there (Jehovah-Shammah). God never speaks outside of who He is. Whether He is foretelling or unveiling, He always reveals His purpose by revealing who He is.

There are two opposing positions concerning prophecy. One says, "We can do anything, and there are no rules." This attitude has helped create divisions because believers don't always take upon themselves sufficient accountability or responsibility for what they have done or said.

The other viewpoint says, "Let's clamp down on anything that doesn't come from the leadership's platform at exactly the right times." This viewpoint contradicts the fact that God chooses the vessel and the time, not man.

These views, therefore, represent two extremes. I believe that it's time for God's people to stop holding to either one of these opposing views and find a way to walk in balance.

The Church needs prophecy. God chose to dwell in man as opposed to simply dwelling with man. Because He wishes to dwell in man, He wants to talk to man. God wants to speak more to His Church, but prophecy will not come until believers begin to take responsibility for what they have said in the name of the Lord.

Being a *People of His Presence* means being released to show forth God. As a result, sound, mature leadership will release believers and allow them to flow in God's presence. In this release, the believer will also need to understand that God has given His leaders instructions to judge and to prove the message. Without accountability and responsibility, God will not give His profound revelation.

A look at both the Old and New Testaments helps give a balanced understanding of prophecy. There is a phrase that has been adopted and is used throughout the Church today; it is "prophetic restoration." I have been looking at this phrase in light of what the whole of Scripture reveals. It is safe to say that Scripture builds line upon line, precept upon precept. The same is true concerning what the Word accomplishes. It builds from the ground up. In the Old Testament, prophecy foretold; in the New Testament, it unveiled; and in the last days, God is revealing Himself.

In the Old Testament, prophecy centered around a man who was the vehicle or prophet, and as a result, the prophets were highly regarded and esteemed. The Old Testament prophets often revealed the word of the Lord to kings and nations.

Some prophets did unusual things to get their message across. Isaiah was seen walking naked through the streets. Hosea was married to a prostitute. Jeremiah wore a yoke. Their message centered on returning to God.

In the New Testament, God's message centered on Jesus.

> *God, who at sundry times and in divers manners spake in time past unto the fathers by the prophets, hath in these last days spoken unto us by his Son, whom he hath appointed heir of all things, by whom also he made the worlds.* Hebrews 1:1-2

This doesn't mean that He did away with the prophets, but rather, He built upon them and unveiled the Son. Now, in our day, there is going to be another emphasis — the Father!

> *Who being the brightness of his glory, and the express image of his person.* Hebrews 1:3

The progression is this: from the Father to man, from man to the Son, and from the Son to the Father. Restoration of prophecy, then, would be returning it to what it was originally. Is it, therefore, the restoration of man? Or is it the restoration of the foundational truth that states: *"In the beginning God."* Prophecy isn't about man; it's about God. God is the center of all things:

> *These are the true sayings of God. And I fell at his feet to worship him. And he said unto me, See thou do it not: I am thy fellowservant, and of thy brethren that have the testimony of Jesus: worship God: for the testimony of Jesus is the spirit of prophecy.*
>
> Revelation 19:9-10

One afternoon while I was studying, the Teacher within me, the Holy Spirit, brought me again to this familiar passage of scripture. I heard Him say, "Look at it again." As I looked, many things began to unfold.

John explains in Revelation 19 that he had had a visitation and had heard a voice come out of the throne, saying, *"Praise our God, all ye his servants, and ye that fear him, both small and great"* (verse 5). This voice, the voice of the Holy Spirit, holds the key to unlocking the eternal truth of prophetic utterance for these last days.

First, it is important to note that there was an angel, a messenger of God, who had a special relationship with the throne of God. John wanted to worship this angel (see verse 10). The angel told John that He was but a *"fellow servant."*

John, we know, was one of the disciples of Jesus. He knew what Jesus looked like, both as man and as He was when He was transfigured upon the mountain. Even so, hearing the words of the angel who had a special relationship with the throne of God caused John to want to fall at his feet to worship him — a mere created being.

This incident, as the Spirit quickened it to me, teaches that there will be a people who, because of their singular relationship with God and the throne, will make a special impact. When they speak, some of those who hear them will fall at their feet and worship them. The messenger told John:

> *See thou do it not: I am thy fellowservant, and of thy brethren that have the testimony of Jesus.*
>
> Revelation 19:10

This messenger brought the *"testimony of Jesus."* In the previous verse John describes hearing *"the true sayings of God."* First, the messenger had spoken to John, revealing true worship:

> *Praise our God, all ye his servants, and ye that fear him, both small and great. And I heard as it were the voice of a great multitude, and as the voice of many waters, and as the voice of mighty thunderings, saying, Alleluia: for the Lord God omnipotent reigneth.*
>
> Revelation 19:5-6

This singular voice now became *"the sound of many,"* as they proclaimed the omnipotence of God and His Kingdom.

The Testimony of Jesus

John then heard the declaration of what was to come:

> *Let us be glad and rejoice, and give honour to him: for the marriage of the Lamb is come, and his wife hath made herself ready. And to her was granted that she should be arrayed in fine linen, clean and white: for the fine linen is the righteousness of saints.*
>
> Revelation 19:7-8

In these last days, true prophecy will show forth the decrees of God that have been in existence since time began. It will prepare and point the way for the return of the King and His Kingdom.

John was also given instruction:

> *And he saith unto me, Write, Blessed are they which are called unto the marriage supper of the Lamb. And he saith unto me, These are the true sayings of God.*
>
> Revelation 19:9

The words of prophecy that are found in Revelation contain one dynamic element — the eternal. Prophecy in these last days will bear one mark and one mark alone, God's eternal name. *"The true sayings of God"* — this is prophecy.

The messenger who spoke to John was speaking forth the sayings of God. It was these sayings that caused John to fall at the angel's feet, and it was to these sayings that the messenger referred when he spoke of *"the testimony of Jesus"* (verse 10).

To understand the full impact of this passage, we will look at the root of the word *testimony,* since much of the messenger's impact was based on *"the testimony of Jesus."*

The word *testimony* comes from the root word *maturia,* which speaks of "one who walks in the personal knowledge of" or "one who speaks with authority as one who knows, intimately." This meaning goes beyond traditional understanding, which simply speaks of "giving witness" or "a testimony that recounts something that has happened." *Testimony,* as used here, denotes "a proclamation that is based on intimate knowledge." Thus, it speaks of John's ability to hear the messenger's voice. The word testimony also comes from the root word *martyr,* which is "a person who is put to death because he or she refuses to denounce his or her personal relationship to a cause, a principle, or a belief." In Revelation 12:17, the Scriptures speak of a war between the dragon and the remnant who have *"the testimony of Jesus,"* indicating that there will be a remnant of the seed of Israel who hold fast during the time of Jacob's trouble to their belief in Yeshua.

The messenger who spoke had an intimate knowledge of God and a relationship with Him. This relationship gave him the authority to speak. We can no longer expect to have God's authority without having a relationship to go along with it. All authority begins and ends within a personal relationship with God.

In the past, I taught that this scripture indicates that when the Spirit of prophecy is present, all may prophesy, and that "testimony" was the content of what was said when this kind of prophecy went forth (i.e., edification, exhortation, comfort, etc.). But this portion of scripture states far more. The messenger who spoke to John did not give a word of edification, exhortation or comfort. He didn't relay a testimony based on previous experience. Therefore, I have to come to the conclusion that it is inadequate to say that this portion of scripture is simply tied to a particular element of prophecy.

In the phrase *"the spirit of prophecy"* there are two distinct words, *"spirit"* and *"prophecy."* As we have established, testimony is not a mere rehearsal or telling of a future event, but rather, it is an intimate relationship. So it is safe to say that the foundation of the spirit of prophecy is the foundation of a personal relationship with God and His authority (throne).

The second word we will focus on is *"spirit,"* which is *pneuma* in Greek and is *ruach* in Hebrew, as found in Isaiah:

> *And there shall come forth a rod out of the stem of Jesse, and a Branch shall grow out of his roots: And the SPIRIT of the LORD shall rest upon him, the SPIRIT of wisdom and understanding, the SPIRIT of counsel and might, the SPIRIT of knowledge and of the fear of the LORD.* Isaiah 11:1-2

Isaiah is speaking of the seven spirits of God. These spirits are the very breath of God, the very essence of who God is *(rucah)*. In light of this understanding, the *"spirit of prophecy"* is the very essence of God Himself. When the messenger spoke, he was speaking forth the very essence of God, with whom he maintained a divine relationship. Therefore, he could speak the eternal true sayings of God.

I stated earlier that prophecy is being restored. The emphasis will be on God and not on man. In the case we have reviewed from Revelation, the messenger first proclaimed that God was to be worshiped. Second, he made known the eternal Kingdom of God. Third, he revealed the eternal things to come. And fourth, he deposited the promises of God. In these last days, prophecy brings into focus the eternal nature of God and the Kingdom of God. Please understand! I am not saying that this present restoration of prophecy will not flow through man, but I am saying that man will not be the primary focus of its message.

There will be an increase of true prophets and of prophecies going forth, as man yields to the purpose of God, and not to his own purpose. What began with the Father, will surely end with the Father.

Prophecy is God! It cannot be swept under the carpet or ignored. It is the declaration of His name, His acts, His judgements and His promises. It is being restored, and will be restored, to the Father, who is the center of all things.

If we walk in true relationship with God, we will reveal the heart of God and the purposes of God. We will be a prophetic people.

Conclusion

We Shall Be Like Him

Beloved, now are we the sons of God, and it doth not yet appear what we shall be: but we know that, when he shall appear, we shall be like him; for we shall see him as he is. 1 John 3:2

In this hour our Beloved is calling us to come to Him. It is the cry of intimacy. Once you respond, you will see Him in all of His glory. When we see Him we are changed. From the beginning of time the Father wanted to have a people whom He could call His own and write His name upon. His desire has not changed. He still wishes to have a people who are willing to surrender all that they are, and who are willing to be fashioned by the Potter's hand into a vessel of honor that is fit for the Master's use.

We are to be a *People of His Presence* — a people who understand who it is that indwells them, and a people who are surrendered to the purposes of God. In this generation there have been "prophetic" movements, with many manifestations and much splendor. Unfortunately, there has been little understanding of the presence of the God who is revealing Himself in this hour through these outpourings. I encourage you not to be content with what you see or feel. Press in deeper to know the One who ignites the flame, causes the winds to blow, and gives the rain from heaven.

Once you have seen Him, you will be like Him. Then, and only then, will you be able to effectively reach out and touch others.

- *Notes* -

- Notes -

- *Notes* -

Books that Motivate Woship

ISBN 1-884369-09-X

Ask for it at your local bookstore,
or order directly from *Cynthia Duggan Ministries* (803) 971-9001

Ministry address:

Cynthia Duggan
P.O. Box 1630
Mt. Pleasant, South Carolina 29465-1630
(803) 971-9001

Tapes are avaliable upon request.